Contents

The Terra-Cotta Warriors: An Army of Clay 3
Comprehension: Recalling Details; Making Inferences; Expressing an Opinion; Critical Thinking
Vocabulary: Understanding Word Meaning; Using Vocabulary in Context
Spelling: Identifying Correct Spelling

The Joy of Camping 13
Comprehension: Recalling Details; Sequencing; Categorizing; Depicting Ideas Graphically
Vocabulary: Understanding Word Meaning; Writing a Definition
Reference Skills: Using a Dictionary
Writing: Descriptive Writing; Writing an Opinion

Mrs. Groggins 23
Comprehension: Recalling Details; Drawing Conclusions; Cause and Effect; Character Analysis; Critical Thinking
Vocabulary: Understanding Word Meaning
Fluency: Reading with Correct Phrasing

Deborah Sampson, Revolutionary Soldier 34
Comprehension: Recalling Details; Critical Thinking; Making Inferences; Interpreting Graphic Information
Vocabulary: Understanding Word Meaning; Synonyms

The Exmoor Pony 45
Comprehension: Recalling Details; Critical Thinking; Categorizing
Vocabulary: Understanding Word Meaning; Using Vocabulary in Context
Phonics/Structural Analysis: Using the Prefix *pre–*
Grammar: Using Adjectives
Writing: Relating Information in Writing

Hercules and the Many-Headed Hydra 55
Comprehension: Recalling Details; Drawing Conclusions; Critical Thinking; Categorizing; Interpreting Information Graphically
Vocabulary: Understanding Word Meaning; Understanding Descriptive Language
Writing: Writing a Creative Story

Northward Bound 66
Comprehension: Recalling Details; Making Inferences; Critical Thinking; Character Analysis
Vocabulary: Understanding Word Meaning
Fluency: Reading Accurately
Writing: Writing a Personal Narrative

A Clever Jester Fools a King 78
Comprehension: Recalling Details; Drawing Conclusions; Critical Thinking; Supporting an Opinion with Facts; Categorizing
Vocabulary: Understanding Word Meaning; Creating Analogies
Grammar: Using Verbs

The Magic Mirror 90
Comprehension: Getting the Main Idea; Recalling Details; Making Inferences; Critical Thinking
Vocabulary: Understanding Word Meaning; Using Vocabulary in Context
Fluency: Reading with Expression
Reference Skills: Using a Dictionary
Writing: Narrative Writing; Writing a Description

Animal Partnerships 99
Comprehension: Recalling Details; Drawing Conclusions; Making Inferences; Critical Thinking; Categorizing
Vocabulary: Understanding Word Meaning; Using a Dictionary
Spelling: Identifying Correct Spelling
Writing: Writing Sentences

The Sausage 110
Comprehension: Recalling Details; Critical Thinking; Getting the Main Idea
Vocabulary: Understanding Word Meaning; Using Vocabulary in Context; Using a Graphic Organizer; Working with Story Elements
Punctuation: Using Apostrophes

Baba Yaga 121
Comprehension: Recalling Details; Drawing Conclusions; Making Inferences; Making a Prediction; Critical Thinking Using a Graphic Organizer; Summarizing
Vocabulary: Understanding Word Meaning; Word Meaning from Context
Fluency: Reading with Intonation

Tracking Form 135

Answer Key 137

The Terra-Cotta Warriors

An Army of Clay

One cool morning in 1974, some Chinese farmers set out with their shovels across their shoulders. They were going to work on the well they had been digging. They spoke and laughed pleasantly among themselves as they walked, but when they reached the site of the well, they became more serious. Each man set his shovel into the soil and began to work quietly. Talking took energy away from the difficult task.

After some time had passed, however, one of the men cried out. "Look at this!" he exclaimed. The others gathered around, intrigued.

"What is it?" asked one of the men.

"It is a bit of pottery," answered another.

"Why, it looks like a face," said the first man. "Perhaps it is part of a statue. We had better report this."

Hearing about what the farmers had found, the government sent a team of archeologists to **excavate** the well. As they began to explore the site, the archeologists found life-sized clay figures. There were warriors, horses, and **chariots**. Ultimately, over 7,000 statues were uncovered.

Those farmers toiling at the well did not know it, but they had stumbled onto one of the world's most amazing archeological discoveries. Who made these **elaborate** statues, and why?

For answers, we must look back more than 2,000 years. At that time, China was ruled by Qin Shi Huang, its first **emperor**, who had become ruler when he was only 13 years old!

Although Qin was not a kind ruler, he was very strong and **effective**. Under his rule, the Great Wall of China was begun. Qin **regulated** trade throughout China and built roads to connect many cities. He improved **communications** by making sure the Chinese used a common language and a uniform system of writing.

Qin was very powerful and wealthy and lived a **lavish** life. He could have anything he wanted. Indeed, the entire country and all within it were under his control. But in spite of his wealth and power, Qin was still a human being, and like all people, he began to grow old. As he aged, he grew fearful of death and began to search for a way to extend his life. He asked his advisors to help him. But even his wisest **counselors** could not stop the march of time.

At last, Qin accepted the fact that he could not live forever. He decided that he would create a magnificent **tomb**. Inside, he would provide all the things he had enjoyed in life. Of course, as emperor, he needed an army. So he had his artists mold thousands of **warriors** from a type of clay called **terra cotta**.

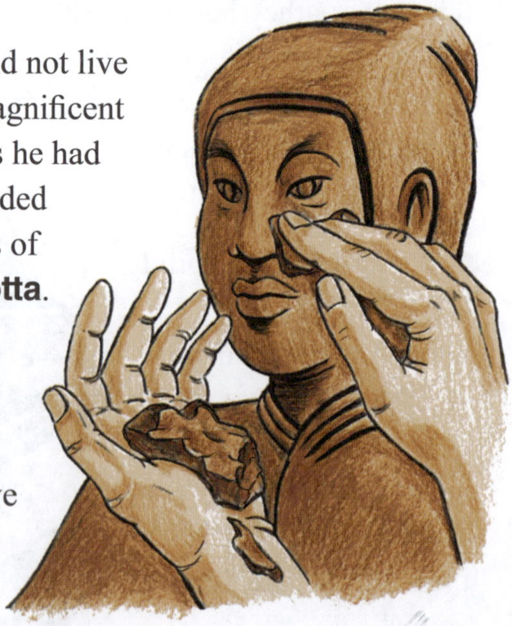

This was an amazing project. No two of the soldiers were alike. Each one was an individual, with a face and expression different from the others. The artists even gave the statues different hairstyles.

The soldiers were wearing a variety of uniforms showing differences in **rank**. There were foot soldiers, **archers**, and generals. Also, the soldiers varied in height with the tallest being over 6 feet 2 inches tall! All the soldiers were outfitted with real weapons.

Once the soldiers were finished, they were placed in battle formation in front of Qin's burial place. Qin believed that the soldiers would protect him in the afterlife.

In addition to the soldiers, there were terra-cotta acrobats in the tomb. The emperor wanted these for entertainment. There were also many servants to wait on him. Life-sized horses and other animals **crafted** from clay were placed in the tomb along with clay fruits and vegetables. It seems that Emperor Qin thought of everything!

It is difficult to imagine the amount of time, effort, and talent required to create this enormous tomb. Its wonders lay hidden from public view for many centuries. The statues, once painted in lifelike colors, faded to their natural clay **hue**. The weapons that once armed the soldiers disappeared. Most likely, they were stolen from the tomb many hundreds of years ago. At some point in time, the wooden roof over the tomb collapsed, and many of the figures were broken.

Archeologists are working to rebuild the figures. They search carefully for tiny **fragments** and glue the figures together with great care. They want to make sure that each figure is **restored** perfectly.

Huge buildings now cover the entire site. These protect the figures from exposure to wind, sun, and rain that could damage the statues.

While hundreds of people work at the site, thousands more come to visit the terra-cotta army every day. It is exciting for people to see these artifacts from the past. However, tourists can accidentally harm the figures. Simply touching or breathing on old and **fragile artifacts** can create damage.

Also, along with crowds of people come food and litter. These items provide a breeding ground for bacteria and mold, which can cause great harm to the figures.

Scientists want tourists to be able to see the figures, but they also want to protect this amazing site. As they continue to explore and learn about the figures, they are working to find ways for tourists to visit the figures without causing harm.

Perhaps someday you will be able to travel to China to visit the terra-cotta warriors. You will see them standing in neat rows, still guarding Emperor Qin, still bravely facing the centuries.

Skills: Recalling Details; Making Inferences

Questions About The Terra-Cotta Warriors

Fill in the circle that best answers each question.

1. The clay figures were placed in the emperor's ______.
   Ⓐ barn
   Ⓑ tomb
   Ⓒ palace
   Ⓓ garden

2. Why did Emperor Qin order his people to make the statues?
   Ⓐ They were to be placed all around his palace as decoration for a big party.
   Ⓑ They were to be placed in his tomb to provide for his needs in the afterlife.
   Ⓒ They were to be part of a museum showing life in China at that time.
   Ⓓ They were to be given as gifts to his most valued friends.

3. Many of the figures were broken when ______.
   Ⓐ a great earthquake rocked the building where the figures are now stored
   Ⓑ the government decided to get rid of the figures
   Ⓒ the wooden roof covering the figures collapsed
   Ⓓ vandals found and destroyed the figures

4. Archeologists are trying to ______.
   Ⓐ sell the figures
   Ⓑ copy the figures
   Ⓒ destroy the figures
   Ⓓ restore the figures

5. The weapons that were with the statues ______.
   Ⓐ are still in working condition
   Ⓑ were probably stolen many years ago
   Ⓒ were broken during the excavation
   Ⓓ are of no interest to archeologists

6. Tourists can harm the figures by ______.
   Ⓐ looking at them
   Ⓑ talking about them
   Ⓒ reading about them
   Ⓓ touching them or breathing on them

Write About the Story

Answer the questions using complete sentences.

1. What other kinds of figures were found with the soldiers?

2. What do you think is the most interesting fact about these figures?

3. How would the statues have looked different had you seen them when they were created?

4. Should tourists be allowed to visit these figures? Explain your answer.

Choose the Right Meaning

Find each bolded word in the story and read the sentence in which it is found. Choose the correct meaning for the word.

1. An **emperor** is similar to ______.
   Ⓐ a king
   Ⓑ a clown
   Ⓒ a scientist
   Ⓓ a carpenter

2. In this story, we learn that **terra cotta** is a kind of ______.
   Ⓐ oil
   Ⓑ clay
   Ⓒ paint
   Ⓓ metal

3. A **warrior** is about the same as ______.
   Ⓐ a bricklayer
   Ⓑ a mechanic
   Ⓒ a soldier
   Ⓓ a painter

4. The word **elaborate** means ______.
   Ⓐ old and damaged
   Ⓑ fancy and ornate
   Ⓒ plain and simple
   Ⓓ brand new

5. A **fragment** is ______.
   Ⓐ a broken piece
   Ⓑ a whole object
   Ⓒ a photograph
   Ⓓ a blueprint

6. Something that is **fragile** is ______.
   Ⓐ flexible and stretchy
   Ⓑ heavy and strong
   Ⓒ sturdy and thick
   Ⓓ easily broken

7. Which of these might you **excavate**?
   Ⓐ your stamp collection
   Ⓑ a burning building
   Ⓒ ancient ruins
   Ⓓ a funny story

8. If a solution to a problem is **effective**, it ______.
   Ⓐ is obvious
   Ⓑ is too hard
   Ⓒ works
   Ⓓ doesn't work

9. The word **regulated** means ______.
   Ⓐ made easy
   Ⓑ found out
   Ⓒ retrained
   Ⓓ controlled

10. Which of these things would be likely to be **restored**?
   Ⓐ an old car
   Ⓑ a sandwich
   Ⓒ a broken window
   Ⓓ a spelling test grade

Which Word Fits?

Complete each sentence using a word from the story.

Word Box

chariots	communication	lavish	counselor	archers
hues	tomb	artifacts	crafted	rank

1. The ________________ advised Allan to take algebra and biology.
2. Lacey used bright, vibrant ________________ to create her painting of the sunset.
3. In Williamsburg, we saw many ________________ from the colonial period.
4. Uncle Bud gave a ________________ party to celebrate his daughter's wedding.
5. The ________________ of the pharaoh is deep inside the pyramid.
6. Helen bought a lovely basket that was ________________ from pine needles.
7. The Romans sometimes used ________________ for travel and for racing.
8. E-mail has made ________________ much easier and more convenient.
9. My grandfather reached the ________________ of general, the highest in the army.
10. The ________________ shot their arrows at the oncoming soldiers.

Write your own sentences using two interesting words from the story.

____

____

____

Fact or Opinion?

A **fact** tells information that is true.
An **opinion** tells about someone's thoughts or feelings.

Write **fact** or **opinion** after each statement.

1. The terra-cotta warriors are very interesting. ______________
2. Emperor Qin was a good emperor. ______________
3. Thousands of tourists visit the terra-cotta warriors each year. ______________
4. The figures include horses and other animals. ______________
5. The horses are the most beautiful figures. ______________
6. The statues were once painted in lifelike colors. ______________
7. It would be fun to be an archeologist. ______________
8. Bacteria and mold can harm the figures. ______________
9. It was silly for the emperor to have these figures made. ______________
10. It is important for people to know about history. ______________

Write one fact and one opinion of your own. Ask a family member to tell which is which.

____

____

____

____

Which Spelling Is Correct?

Circle the correct spelling for each word.

individual	individule	individial
soldere	soldier	solldier
statue	stachue	stasue
unaform	uniform	uneform
expresion	expreshun	expression
counsellor	counseler	counselor
serias	serrious	serious
energy	ennergy	energie
axidental	accidental	accidenttal
guarding	garding	gaurding

Write sentences using the correct spellings of three words from the list.

1. ______________________________

2. ______________________________

3. ______________________________

The Joy of Camping

Ah, the great outdoors! Whether you are hiking through the magnificent redwoods of Northern California, sleeping under the brilliant stars of the Texas sky, or watching the sun rise across the rocky cliffs of Maine, experiencing the outdoor world can be inspiring, thrilling, and deeply satisfying. And one of the best ways to enjoy the **abundant** gifts of the natural world is simple, inexpensive, and available to almost everyone. Let's go camping!

Many people who have never camped outdoors sometimes imagine that camping is uncomfortable, difficult, and complicated. But with just a little preparation, planning, and experience, camping can become a favorite pastime. It is a great way for friends and family to enjoy time together and to restore the important ties between people and nature.

Gathering Your Equipment

When you camp, you create a "home away from home" in the fresh air. You don't need a lot of fancy equipment to enjoy camping.

Sleeping Area

You will need a tent that is large enough for your family. Practice setting up the tent at home to make sure you are familiar with the process before you go camping.

Each person also needs a sleeping bag. For summer camping in most locations around the United States, a fairly lightweight bag will **suffice**.

Sleeping pads add to the comfort of the camping experience. These come in a variety of materials and a wide range of prices.

Sleeping Area

tarp

tent (Don't forget tent stakes and a hammer.)

sleeping bag for each camper

sleeping pad for each camper

Camp Kitchen

The basic kitchen kit begins with a two-burner propane stove, available at any camping supply store. You will also need some cookware and enough dishes to serve all the campers in your group. Many of the items you'll need for your camp kitchen can be found around the house or at a discount store.

Camp Kitchen Kit

- *propane stove*
- *extra propane bottles*
- *two saucepans*
- *one frying pan*
- *large spoon*
- *spatula*
- *paring knife*
- *small cutting board*
- *cup, plate, bowl, knife, fork, and spoon for each camper*
- *dishpan for washing up*
- *dishcloth or sponge*
- *old dish towels*
- *hot pads*
- *can opener*
- *aluminum foil*
- *zipper-lock plastic bags*
- *matches*
- *large plastic bin to hold all kitchen items*

Personal Care

You will also need to bring along the items you need to stay clean and healthy.

Personal Care Kit

- *hand-washing can*
- **biodegradable** *soap*
- *dishpan (for hand-washing or bathing)*
- *collapsible bucket*
- *towel for each camper*
- *clothesline and clothespins*
- *sunscreen*
- *insect repellent*
- *moisturizing lotion*
- *a small mirror*
- *toothpaste*
- *toilet paper*
- *first-aid kit*
- **prescription** *medicines*
- *small plastic bin to hold all personal care items*

Drinking Water

Most developed campgrounds offer campers a **potable** water supply. Potable water is water that is clean and safe to drink. However, it is always a good idea to bring your own drinking water unless you are certain that clean water is available at the campground. A water bottle or **canteen** for each camper is **essential**.

Setting Up Camp

At most campgrounds, you are required to register when you arrive. If you have a choice of campsites, look around to find a good one.

Sleeping Area

Once you find a site that you like, it's time to set up camp. Your first job is to set up your tent. Remove all sticks and rocks from the area. Spread a tarp over the area where your tent will sit. Set up the tent and be sure to stake it down firmly, even if the weather is mild. Otherwise, a sudden **gust** of wind can blow your tent away!

Roll out your sleeping pad and bag on the tent floor. Place your flashlight near the head of your sleeping bag so that you can find it in the night. A water bottle (tightly closed!) is a nice item to have nearby as well. When you have your sleeping area all arranged, be sure to completely zip the doors and windows of your tent closed to keep mosquitoes out!

Camp Kitchen

Next, you are ready to set up your camp kitchen. Spread your tablecloth on the table and set up your propane stove. Place your bin of cooking equipment in a handy location near the table. Place your coolers with food and drink in a shady location to keep them cool. If bear-proof boxes are provided for food storage, use them!

Personal Care Area

Select an area for hand-washing that is near the kitchen area. String a clothesline between two trees so that you can hang towels or swimsuits to dry. Make sure that the clothesline is located where people will not run into it while moving around the campsite.

This is also a good place to locate the first-aid kit. A stump or large rock could provide a handy surface for this purpose. Fill your bucket with water and place it nearby. Set up the hand-washing system as illustrated in the picture.

When you want to wash your hands, dip the can into the bucket of water without ***submerging*** *your dirty hands in the water. Use the stream of water from the can and* ***biodegradable*** *soap to wash your hands. This system keeps your water supply fresh and clean for the next camper.*

Firewood

Next, you'll need some firewood for a campfire. If gathering wood is illegal at your campground, you must buy it at the camp store. If gathering dead and downed wood is permitted, go on a firewood-hunting expedition and bring in a good supply of wood for your campsite. Pile the wood safely away from the campfire ring and where no one will trip over the wood or **gouge** his or her legs on sharp branches.

Extras

Bring along a folding camp chair for each camper. Set these up around the campfire ring. Also, be sure to bring a camera and some film to record the beautiful scenery and capture images of local wildlife. A sketchbook and some colored pencils, a deck of cards, and a book of campfire tales are great for relaxing in camp after a long day of hiking, fishing, or swimming.

Follow the Rules

Being a responsible camper requires that you follow the rules of the campground. Be sure to store food as directed, especially in areas where bears are active.

Always place trash in designated **receptacles**, or carry it out with you. Do not burn food, plastic, or aluminum in your campfire.

Make sure that you leave your campsite in **pristine** condition for the next campers. Just before leaving the site, make a final check to be certain that your campfire is completely out. Pour water on the ashes just to be safe!

The next time your family plans a vacation, suggest a camping trip. It is fun for all ages, and there are wonderful campgrounds all across the country. If possible, log on to the National Park Service Web site at www.nps.gov to find an exciting and interesting place to explore. Happy camping to all!

Questions About The Joy of Camping

Fill in the circle that best answers each question.

1. You should practice setting up your tent ______.
   Ⓐ after you select your campsite
   Ⓑ before your first camping trip
   Ⓒ after you gather firewood
   Ⓓ before you purchase it

2. You should zip up your tent ______.
   Ⓐ after you arrange your sleeping bag
   Ⓑ before you choose a campsite
   Ⓒ before you get out of the car
   Ⓓ after you gather firewood

3. What is the first thing you should do after choosing a campsite?
   Ⓐ run and play
   Ⓑ gather firewood
   Ⓒ eat some snacks
   Ⓓ remove sticks and rocks from the tent area

4. You should only gather firewood after ______.
   Ⓐ taking a nap in your tent
   Ⓑ looking to see if a ranger is in the area
   Ⓒ making sure that firewood gathering is allowed
   Ⓓ checking to see if other campers are gathering wood

5. The last thing you should do before you leave your campsite is ______.
   Ⓐ take a picture
   Ⓑ take down your tent
   Ⓒ roll up your sleeping bag
   Ⓓ make sure your campfire is completely out

6. This article is mostly about ______.
   Ⓐ cooking outdoors
   Ⓑ the National Park Service
   Ⓒ the hiking trails in California
   Ⓓ camping as a great recreational activity

Making a List

Under each heading, make a list of as many items as you can remember from the article. Don't peek!

When you have finished making your list, reread the article and add items you may have forgotten.

Sleeping Area

Camp Kitchen

Personal Care Area

Extras

Choose the Right Meaning

Find each bolded word in the article and read the sentence in which it is found. Choose the correct meaning for the word.

1. The word **suffice** means ______.
   - Ⓐ enough
   - Ⓑ too small
   - Ⓒ attractive
   - Ⓓ uncomfortable

2. The word **gouge** means to ______.
   - Ⓐ weigh or measure
   - Ⓑ laugh or giggle
   - Ⓒ dig or scrape
   - Ⓓ pull or tug

3. The word **submerge** means to ______.
   - Ⓐ hide
   - Ⓑ float
   - Ⓒ put under water
   - Ⓓ bury in the ground

4. A **pastime** is ______.
   - Ⓐ something that happened in the past
   - Ⓑ a hobby or recreational activity
   - Ⓒ something that is late or overdue
   - Ⓓ a task or chore

5. An item that is **essential** is ______.
   - Ⓐ very common
   - Ⓑ just for fun
   - Ⓒ very soft
   - Ⓓ necessary

6. A **gust** is ______.
   - Ⓐ a sudden blast of wind
   - Ⓑ a constant breeze
   - Ⓒ a gentle puff
   - Ⓓ a rainstorm

7. Which of these not **biodegradable**?
   - Ⓐ paper
   - Ⓑ banana peel
   - Ⓒ chicken bones
   - Ⓓ aluminum pie tin

8. If you have an **abundant** supply, you have ______.
   - Ⓐ a few
   - Ⓑ many
   - Ⓒ not enough for all
   - Ⓓ the last of the bunch

9. Something that is **collapsible** is ______.
   - Ⓐ easy to close
   - Ⓑ side by side, or parallel
   - Ⓒ able to be broken down or folded up
   - Ⓓ something that works together with something else

10. A **bin** is ______.
    - Ⓐ a bundle
    - Ⓑ a fenced-in area
    - Ⓒ something that has two parts
    - Ⓓ a box or receptacle for storing things

Definitions

Use a dictionary to look up each word taken from the article.
Read the dictionary definition. Write the word meaning in your own words.

1. **canteen**

___

2. **pristine**

___

3. **prescription**

___

4. **receptacle**

___

5. **potable**

___

Draw a picture of these words:

receptacle

canteen

Map It!

Pretend that you are a bird perched on a tree above a campsite like the one described in the article. Draw a map of the campsite from this perspective.

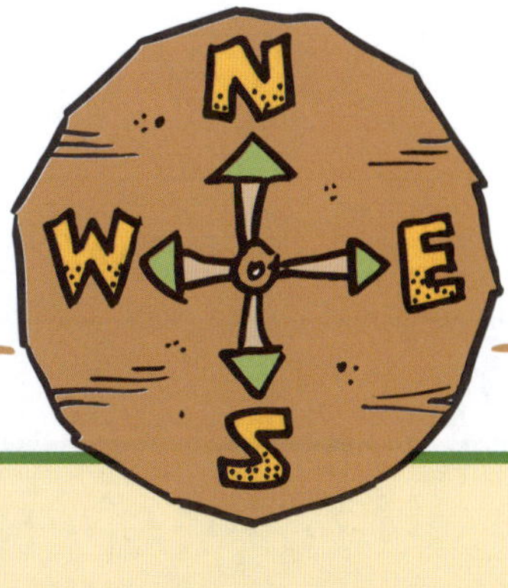

The Best Place to Camp

Write a paragraph about the place you would most like to camp. Be sure to fully describe the place and explain why it would be the best camping spot for you. This can be a place that you have already visited or a new place that you would like to explore. It can even be your own backyard!

Mrs. Groggins

Mrs. Groggins was a teacher. She had been a teacher for a great many years. In fact, none of the other teachers at Bellwood School knew just how long Glenda Groggins had been ensconced in her sixth-grade classroom. All they knew was that she had been there long before any of them came to work at Bellwood. It seemed no living person could remember a time when Mrs. Groggins was not the sixth-grade teacher at Bellwood School.

Mrs. Groggins was a dreadful woman, and her face seemed to have been formed to fit her personality. It was narrow and tight, and wore a perpetually grumpy expression. Her nose was long and hard, and appeared exceptionally bony. Were it not for her particularly large nostrils, one might wonder how she managed to get enough air to survive. Her mouth was tense and **puckered**, and the only time she opened it was to shriek at her class. But as we shall see, this was seldom necessary.

In all her years of teaching, Mrs. Groggins had never extracted the least bit of enjoyment from her profession. In truth, she despised it. All the children, all their questions, all their noise, were too much for her **brittle** nerves to bear.

"Silence!" she would scream. "I need silence!" And the **menacing** sound of her voice sent children cowering to their seats.

Silence was so important to Mrs. Groggins that she did not allow speaking in her classroom. She herself rarely spoke, preferring to write her instructions on the blackboard for the children to read. Her usual method of showing disapproval of the students' behavior was to rake her long fingernails across the blackboard. Then she would glare menacingly at any boy who made the mistake of rattling his papers and pencils about, or any girl who foolishly opened her mouth to allow a sound to escape.

This particular day was one of the worst days of the year for Mrs. Groggins. It was the first day of school. She headed toward her classroom wondering what kind of rabble awaited her this year. As she spied them standing in the hallway, she was not at all surprised by the looks of them. They were, after all, girls and boys like all the others. They played games, laughed, and talked as they jostled their way into the classroom. These behaviors were, in Mrs. Groggins' view, simply **unendurable**.

With a grimace of distaste, she walked deliberately to the front of the classroom and stopped in front of the blackboard. She turned to face the students and, using only the force of her icy glare, rendered all the children as silent and still as statues.

She picked up a piece of chalk and began to write:

Mrs. Groggins
Rules of the Classroom

Under this she wrote the number 1, followed by a period.

There is to be no talking at any time. You will follow all directions or be punished.

That was it. These were the only rules. She turned to face the class again, her **ruthless** gaze sweeping over the frightened children. On the faces of the fastest readers, a **stunned** look of disbelief was just beginning to register. The look quickly spread over the whole of the classroom. Seeing that look provoked a feeling of satisfaction in Mrs. Groggins' shriveled heart. As she turned back to the blackboard, she allowed herself a teeny, tiny smile.

She again applied the chalk to the board.

Write a five-paragraph essay describing what you did on your summer vacation.

The students began to take out papers and pencils, doing so as quietly as possible for fear that the slightest noise might send this **maniacal** teacher into a rampage, as indeed it would have. For her part, Mrs. Groggins marched back to her desk where she sat down, opened her desk drawer, and retrieved a very ripe banana. She carefully peeled the rotten-looking skin off the fruit, then took up a novel and began to read. As she read, the smell of the banana permeated the overly warm classroom. But the children dared not complain. Indeed, they barely lifted their pencils from their papers or their eyes from their work.

After an hour had passed, Mrs. Groggins sensed that the children had finished the assigned task. They had begun to shift slightly in their seats, though none were so bold as to speak or even raise a hand. Marking her place in the book with the folded banana skin, Mrs. Groggins stood up and walked again to the blackboard.

Exchange papers with the person next to you

she wrote, and then went back to her reading. The students dutifully read each other's accounts of the summer, lulled almost to stupefaction from inactivity and boredom. At last, the slow-moving hands of the classroom clock clicked around to the blessed moment of recess. The children filed tensely out of the classroom, bursting with eagerness to be out in the fresh air, talking and moving.

Mrs. Groggins looked out the window at the youngsters running and playing on the green grass of the schoolyard and shuddered. She closed the blinds with a metallic snap, and turned to survey her empty classroom.

"Good job, old girl," she congratulated herself. "You've got them just where you want them. You won't have a bit of trouble with this group of grubs!" And she sat kneading her temples in silence until the bell rang signaling the end of recess.

As soon as the children came back into the classroom, however, things began to unravel. It seemed to Mrs. Groggins that all the progress she had made with the class that morning had been lost. The intimidation which had seemed so complete was eroding. Why, the children were actually whispering among themselves, talking aloud even! And here and there she actually thought she heard a giggle.

Disbelieving, Mrs. Groggins skated to the front of the room and whirled to face the students. She trained upon them her most **diabolical** expression. But the children ignored her! They continued their conversations, and now some of them were rising from their seats and moving around the classroom! They were sharpening pencils, taking books from the shelves, and chattering loudly. She raked her nails wildly across the blackboard to get their attention, but the noise only grew louder. Some of the little maggots had the audacity to laugh out loud!

"Silence!" she wailed. "I require silence!" But if anything, the decibel level in the room increased. The children were completely out of her control.

In all her years of teaching, Mrs. Groggins had never lost command of a classroom in this way. Why, children were always afraid of her, and that fear had kept them in check. She stood, helpless, at the front of the classroom, shrieking frantically, but to no avail. She felt her heart pounding. The first prickling of **hysterical** tears stung her eyes. She began to sway on her narrow feet, certain that her head was about to explode, hearing the sounds of the children's squeals and laughter echoing ever louder in her ringing ears. . . .

Suddenly, all was silent. Mrs. Groggins sat up, a cold sweat trickling down her backbone. She blinked her eyes at the total darkness in which she found herself, and listened in amazement to the utter silence that surrounded her. She could feel, rather than hear, the pounding of her heart begin to subside. As she wiped away the beads of perspiration that jeweled her forehead, relief began to spread through her body.

"It was just a dream," she squeaked, startling herself with the sound of her own voice. It had all been a **hideous** dream, a nightmare of the worst sort imaginable!

As her thoughts swam into focus, Mrs. Groggins breathed a whistling sigh of relief through her long flutelike nose.

"A nightmare, nothing more," she thought as she lay back on her pillow. But she tossed and turned, unable to fall asleep, the distressing images of her dream playing again and again in her mind's eye.

At last, just before daybreak, Mrs. Groggins rose creakily from her bed and shuffled down the hall to her little study. There she drew a sheet of paper from her desk and began to write:

To the Superintendent of the Bellwood School District:

I hereby resign from my position as sixth-grade teacher, effective immediately.

Signed,
Mrs. Groggins

She sealed the letter in an envelope, stamped it, and dropped it into the mailbox on her front porch. Then, drawing her robe tightly around her sticklike body, she nearly danced up the stairs, jumped into bed, rolled up in the covers, and dropped into a deep and peaceful slumber.

Questions About Mrs. Groggins

Fill in the circle that best answers each question.

1. What day was described in the story as "the worst day of the year"?
   Ⓐ the last day of school
   Ⓑ the first day of school
   Ⓒ Halloween
   Ⓓ Valentine's Day

2. What did Mrs. Groggins do when she wanted to get the children's attention?
   Ⓐ She rang a bell.
   Ⓑ She lit a firecracker.
   Ⓒ She turned out the lights.
   Ⓓ She raked her fingernails across the blackboard.

3. What did Mrs. Groggins do while the children were working on their assignment?
   Ⓐ She read a book and ate a banana.
   Ⓑ She read a magazine and ate a cookie.
   Ⓒ She read the newspaper and ate a pear.
   Ⓓ She ate an apple and played a computer game.

4. How did the children feel when it was time for recess?
   Ⓐ They felt disappointed.
   Ⓑ They felt too tired to play.
   Ⓒ They felt happy and relieved.
   Ⓓ They felt confused and did not know what to do.

5. What happened when the children returned from recess?
   Ⓐ They went quietly back to work.
   Ⓑ They lined up and went to the library.
   Ⓒ They laughed and talked and misbehaved.
   Ⓓ They cleaned the classroom from top to bottom.

6. How did you know that Mrs. Groggins felt happy after she wrote her letter of resignation?
   Ⓐ She shouted, "Hooray!"
   Ⓑ She whistled a cheery tune.
   Ⓒ She smiled a little smile.
   Ⓓ She danced up the stairs.

Write About the Story

Complete each sentence to explain why certain events happened in the story.

Mrs. Groggins demanded silence from her students because

____

____.

Mrs. Groggins did not like the looks of her new class because

____

____.

Mrs. Groggins glared meanly at the children because

____

____.

Mrs. Groggins woke up with her heart pounding because

____

____.

Mrs. Groggins wrote a letter because

____

____.

Write as many adjectives as you can think of that describe **Mrs. Groggins**.

____________________ ____________________

____________________ ____________________

____________________ ____________________

____________________ ____________________

Colorful Adjectives

The story of Mrs. Groggins is full of wonderfully vivid **adjectives** that help paint a picture in the reader's mind.

Find the **noun** that each of the adjectives below describes. Then match the adjective with its meaning by writing the letter on the line. The first one has been done for you.

1. puckered mouth ____ h ____
2. brittle ______________ ______
3. hysterical ______________ ______
4. unendurable ______________ ______
5. hideous ______________ ______
6. maniacal ______________ ______
7. diabolical ______________ ______
8. menacing ______________ ______
9. ruthless ______________ ______
10. stunned ______________ ______

a. wicked; cruel

b. unnaturally excited; out of control

c. having no mercy

d. shocked; overwhelmed

e. threatening

f. easily broken

g. unbearable

h. wrinkled; drawn up into folds

i. raving; insane

j. frightful; horrible

Vivid Verbs

An author makes a story come alive by using vivid **verbs** to describe the action. For example, think about how much more descriptive it is to say "She **witnessed** the accident" than to say "She **saw** the accident."

Read each phrase below from the story. Use context to help you choose the correct meaning for the bolded verb. Write the meaning on the line.

1. …had been **ensconced** in her sixth-grade classroom.

   ____

2. …had never **extracted** the least bit of enjoyment from her profession.

   ____

3. In truth, she **despised** it.

   ____

4. …her voice sent children **cowering** to their seats.

   ____

5. …they **jostled** their way into the classroom.

   ____

6. …her icy glare, **rendered** all the children as silent….

   ____

7. Seeing that look **provoked** a feeling of satisfaction….

   ____

8. …the smell of the banana **permeated** the overly warm classroom.

   ____

9. …**lulled** almost to stupefaction from inactivity and boredom.

   ____

10. …the pounding of her heart begin to **subside**.

    ____

spread through	quieted; hushed	cringing; shrinking	hated
taken out	caused to be	settled securely	
elbowing; pushing	brought about; triggered	decrease; become less	

Sense from Nonsense

Change one word in each silly sentence to create a new sentence that makes sense.

1. Liza led the pledge of allegiance to the class.

    ___

2. Rod and Jane passed out math spoons to the class.

    ___

3. When the pizza rang for recess, all the children ran outside.

    ___

4. The teacher told the students to destroy each other's papers.

    ___

5. At the basketball game, many parents sat in the bathtubs and cheered.

    ___

Create two silly sentences of your own. Ask a friend or family member to change your silly sentences so they make sense.

1. ___

    ___

2. ___

    ___

Fluency: Reading with Correct Phrasing

Read the poem below three times.

- Practice reading in natural phrases.
- Pay attention to punctuation marks.
- Pause for breath when you see a comma or period.
- Add extra emphasis to lines that end with exclamation points.

Read the poem aloud to someone who will think it's funny. Be sure to explain about **Mrs. Groggins**, so that the person understands the poem.

Mrs. Groggins' Creed

Here is all you must know to succeed in my school.
I have only one simple, unbreakable rule:

(I hope you're all listening, especially you boys!)
Be quiet. Be silent. Don't make ANY noise.

You will zipper your lip from September to June.
Don't whisper a word or hum a small tune.

Don't rustle. Don't wiggle. Don't let your chair squeak.
If you laugh, you'll be put on detention all week.

You will stifle each sniffle and cancel each cough.
If you feel a burp coming, you must choke it right off!

So eliminate giggles, forget about snuffling.
Finger-tapping's forbidden and so is foot-shuffling.

Don't move and don't talk, and don't think about sneezing.
In fact...

I'd prefer that you even stop breathing!

Deborah Sampson

Revolutionary Soldier

When Deborah Sampson was a young girl, she could never have imagined that monuments would someday be built in her honor. She would not have believed that she would be remembered and celebrated more than 200 years after her birth. Indeed, as a child, Deborah was so poor that she hardly had time to think about anything except the daily struggle to stay alive.

Deborah's family had always been poor and just barely managed to **make ends meet**. Then, Deborah's father—a ship's captain—was lost at sea. Or perhaps he simply abandoned his wife and seven small children. At any rate, Deborah's mother was left alone, a **widow** with no means to support her large family. The children who were old enough to work, including Deborah who was only 6 years old, were sent to live and work in the homes of strangers.

Deborah was "hired out" as a helper to an old woman who was a feeble **invalid**. Deborah's work was hard for such a young person. The old lady's niece, who also lived in the home, was cruel to Deborah and used her harshly. Deborah tried not to complain, as she understood how important it was for her to earn her own keep. She knew her mother could not afford to care for her. But she was miserable and exhausted all the time, and barely got enough to eat.

A good-hearted minister who was a friend of the Sampson family took pity on Deborah. He could see that her situation was a difficult one. He found her a new placement with a kind farm family by the name of Thomas. Deborah agreed to stay with the Thomas family for 10 years in exchange for her room and board.

Deborah loved the Thomas family, and they loved her. She worked hard on the family farm and spent what little free time she had learning to read and write. She was not able to go to school because her helping hands were needed in the Thomas home. But when the older boys were sent to school, Deborah pestered them to repeat their lessons at the end of each day. In this determined way, Deborah was able to obtain an education.

When Deborah was eighteen, it was time for her to leave the Thomas house. Mr. and Mrs. Thomas found Deborah a position as a schoolteacher. She also made extra money by hiring herself out to do spinning and weaving.

One of the places where she often worked was Sproats Tavern. The men who gathered at this tavern talked about the news of the day which—in 1770's Massachusetts—was mostly about the Revolutionary War. The old men talked of politics while the young men swapped stories of their exploits in General Washington's army.

As Deborah sat at the spinning wheel in the back room of the tavern, she listened to these tales with fascination. She wished that she might experience such grand adventures. She was envious of the freedom that young men took for granted. She **resented** the restrictions placed upon young women of her time. She was tired of housework and wanted to take part in the important events that were swirling around her.

Finally, Deborah decided to take action. She secretly made herself a suit of men's clothing. Then she cut off her hair and went off to join the army. She walked through the night to a neighboring town where her face was less familiar. There she enlisted under the name Robert Shurtliff.

Deborah's disguise was enhanced by the fact that she stood five feet eight inches tall, which was taller than the average man of the day and a most unusual height for a woman. The hard work of a lifetime had given her a strong back and well-developed muscles. She could march, work, and fight as well as any of the men in her company.

At that time, army life was not as orderly as it is today. There were no physical exams required for enlistment. Soldiers camped in the fields and woods, sleeping in haystacks and barns and wherever they could find some shelter. They generally slept in their clothes and took care of themselves as best they could.

Deborah got along well with her fellows, but she kept to herself and had little to say. She was viewed as a bashful young boy, but a good soldier nonetheless.

Deborah's unit was involved in several skirmishes. In one fight, she was injured twice. The first injury was a slash to the forehead and the second a musket ball through the thigh. After the battle, she allowed the doctor to dress the cut on her head, but she did not tell the doctor about the bullet wound. Instead, she limped away from the hospital and hid in a cave. There she used her own knife to dig the musket ball out of her leg. When she had recovered her strength, she went back to her company.

By this time, the war was coming to an end, and "Robert Shurtliff" was honorably discharged from the army. Still wearing men's clothing, Deborah returned to her family. Although shocked and surprised by her exploits, the family welcomed her home.

While visiting with relatives, Deborah met a man named Benjamin Gannett. The two hit it off and were soon married. The couple had three children. Then they adopted a little girl whose parents had died. Deborah must surely have had sympathy for the poor little girl because of her own early experiences.

The Gannett family was very poor. Deborah's friends—including the famous Paul Revere—helped her obtain a **pension** from the military for her services. This military pension was a great help, but still not enough to live comfortably. Seeking a way to help support her family, Deborah agreed to cooperate on a book about her life. The book was full of lies and **exaggerations**. Worse, it earned little money.

Desperate to help her family, Deborah decided to go on a speaking tour. This was wildly **out of the ordinary** for women of this time. In fact, Deborah was one of the first women to engage in public speaking. She dressed in a **military** uniform and gave lectures about her unusual experiences.

People were very curious about this brave and **controversial** woman, and her lectures were well-attended. Although they did not make her wealthy, they did bring in enough income to ease the family's poverty.

In the final years of her life, Deborah lived with her son and his wife in a fine home in Sharon, Massachusetts. She died there in 1827 at the age of 67.

There is an interesting footnote to Deborah's story. In 1983, she was recognized as the Official State **Heroine** by the governor of Massachusetts. Her uncommon courage and fierce independence secured her rightful place among America's founding heroes.

Questions About
Deborah Sampson
Revolutionary Soldier

Fill in the circle that best answers each question.

1. Why did Deborah have to leave home and go to work?
   Ⓐ Her mother did not want to take care of her.
   Ⓑ Both of her parents had died in an accident.
   Ⓒ Her mother could not support the family.
   Ⓓ Her father wanted her to learn responsibility.

2. How could you tell that Deborah was a determined person?
   Ⓐ She learned to sew.
   Ⓑ She learned to work hard.
   Ⓒ She worked in a tavern.
   Ⓓ She learned to read and write.

3. Why did Deborah go to a neighboring town to enlist in the army?
   Ⓐ She did not want to be recognized.
   Ⓑ She thought it would be more fun.
   Ⓒ Her friends were enlisting there.
   Ⓓ She wanted to take a walk.

4. Why did Deborah go on a lecture tour?
   Ⓐ Her family needed the money.
   Ⓑ She wanted to become famous.
   Ⓒ She wanted to make new friends.
   Ⓓ She wanted to become president.

5. Who helped Deborah obtain a pension for her military service?
   Ⓐ John Adams
   Ⓑ Paul Revere
   Ⓒ Thomas Jefferson
   Ⓓ George Washington

6. Who was Robert Shurtliff?
   Ⓐ a friend that Deborah met in the army
   Ⓑ the owner of the tavern where she worked
   Ⓒ the identity Deborah took on when she became a soldier
   Ⓓ the kindly minister who got Deborah a better place to work

Build a Story

Fill in the blanks with a word from the story.

Deborah Sampson went to work when she was only ________________ years old. Her life was very ________________. When she grew up, she became a ________________. Sometimes she would ________________ and ________________ to make extra money.

Deborah sometimes wished that she had been born a ________________. She wanted to have the ________________ that men enjoyed. She decided that she would pretend to be a ________________ and join the ________________. She cut her ________________ and made a ________________ for herself. She was as good at ________________ and ________________ as any other soldier. Once, she was shot in the ________________. She used her ________________ to remove the musket ball.

When the war was over, Deborah went home and got married. She had ________________ children. She also adopted a little ________________. Deborah died at the age of ________________.

In 1983, Deborah Sampson became the Official Heroine of the Commonwealth of Massachusetts. Why do you think she was chosen for this honor?

____

____

____

Skills: Understanding Word Meaning

Choose the Right Meaning

Find each bolded word in the story and read the sentence in which it is found. Choose the correct meaning for the word.

1. Which activity is an **invalid** most likely to do?
   - Ⓐ lie in bed
   - Ⓑ go ice-skating
   - Ⓒ run a marathon
   - Ⓓ swim in the ocean

2. A **pension** is likely to be received by ______.
   - Ⓐ a prisoner
   - Ⓑ a retired person
   - Ⓒ a homemaker
   - Ⓓ a student

3. A **widow** is a person ______.
   - Ⓐ who has no home
   - Ⓑ whose friend has died
   - Ⓒ whose husband has died
   - Ⓓ who has never been married

4. Which of the following is an **exaggeration**?
   - Ⓐ I learned to shoot a musket.
   - Ⓑ I carried the musket all day.
   - Ⓒ I outran the musket shot.
   - Ⓓ I heard a loud musket shot.

5. A **heroine** is ______.
   - Ⓐ a woman who is honored for her courage
   - Ⓑ a man who is honored for his courage
   - Ⓒ a beautiful woman
   - Ⓓ a handsome man

6. What do you do if you **make ends meet**?
   - Ⓐ tie the ends of a rope together
   - Ⓑ make a perfect circle with a drawing tool
   - Ⓒ get back to the place you started
   - Ⓓ have just enough money to get by

7. Which of these is **out of the ordinary** today?
   - Ⓐ a woman in the army
   - Ⓑ a woman giving speeches
   - Ⓒ a woman as president of the United States
   - Ⓓ a woman flying on the space shuttle

8. Which of Deborah's actions was **controversial**?
   - Ⓐ spinning and weaving in a tavern
   - Ⓑ serving as a soldier in the army
   - Ⓒ taking care of a feeble invalid
   - Ⓓ adopting a child

9. The word **military** has to do with ____.
   - Ⓐ sermons in church
   - Ⓑ college classes
   - Ⓒ the movement of birds
   - Ⓓ the armed forces

10. The word **resented** means ______.
    - Ⓐ felt insulted
    - Ⓑ felt eager
    - Ⓒ felt tired
    - Ⓓ felt certain

Make a Match

Use a word from the word box to complete each pair of **synonyms**, or words that mean about the same thing. The bolded words in the items are in the story. The sentence in which you find each word will provide a clue to its meaning.

Word Box

traded	weak	memorial	gun	shy
jealous	speech	leave	fight	adventure

1. **Bashful** means about the same as ______________________.
2. **Skirmish** means about the same as ______________________.
3. **Envious** means about the same as ______________________.
4. **Swapped** means about the same as ______________________.
5. **Exploit** means about the same as ______________________.
6. **Monument** means about the same as ______________________.
7. **Feeble** means about the same as ______________________.
8. **Lecture** means about the same as ______________________.
9. **Abandon** means about the same as ______________________.
10. **Musket** means about the same as ______________________.

Fact or Opinion?

A **fact** tells information that is true.
An **opinion** tells about someone's thoughts or feelings.

Write **fact** or **opinion** after each statement.

1. Deborah Sampson fought in the Revolutionary War. ________________
2. Everyone should serve in the military. ________________
3. Deborah was the bravest woman who ever lived. ________________
4. Deborah was one of seven children. ________________
5. Deborah went to work when she was a young girl. ________________
6. Children should never have to do any work. ________________
7. Deborah became a schoolteacher. ________________
8. Deborah knew how to spin and weave. ________________
9. It would be fun to learn how to spin and weave. ________________
10. Deborah Sampson is the most important woman in American history. ________________

Write one fact and one opinion of your own. Ask a family member to tell which is which.

____

____

____

____

Reading a Timeline

Read the timeline of Deborah Sampson's life.
Use information in the story to fill in the missing dates.

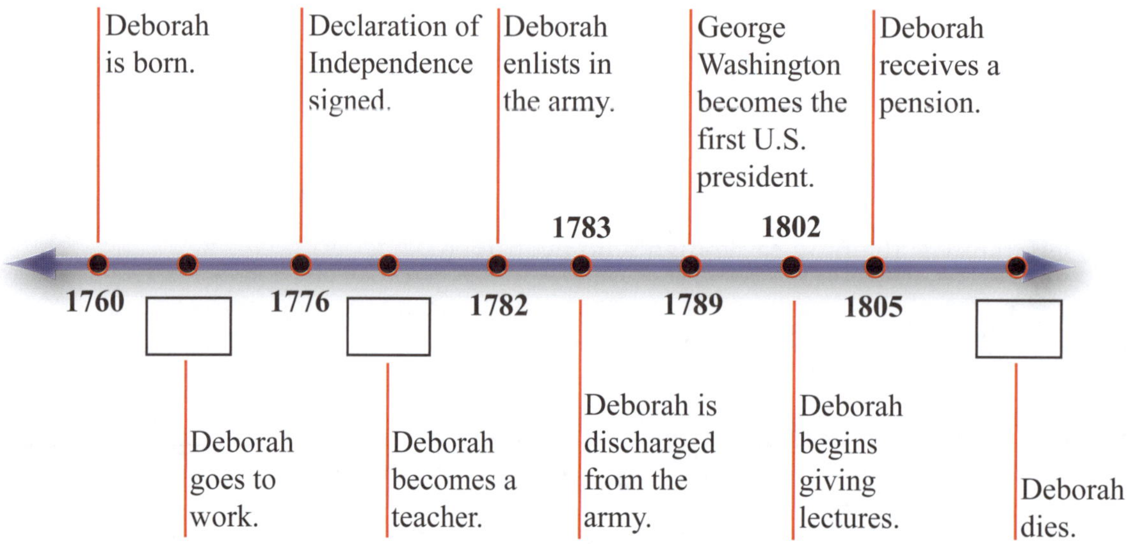

Answer the questions using information from the timeline.

1. How old was Deborah when the Declaration of Independence was signed? ________________

2. How old was Deborah when she joined the army? ________________

3. Was George Washington sworn in as president before or after Deborah left the army? ________________

4. Did Deborah work as a schoolteacher before or after she joined the army? ________________

The Exmoor Pony

When we think of **prehistoric** mammals, we often think of the woolly mammoth or perhaps the saber-toothed tiger. Of course, these fascinating animals have been **extinct** for many years. But did you know that there were also prehistoric horses? One of these horses, the Exmoor pony, has managed to survive. These small, hardy horses still roam the hills of Britain today.

The Exmoor ponies came to Britain over 100,000 years ago, probably walking across a low plain in an area that is now the English Channel, which separates Great Britain from Europe's mainland. When the land changed and the channel appeared, the ponies became isolated. For several thousand years, they had no contact with other horses and bred only with each other. As a result, the Exmoor pony is a very pure breed.

How did the Exmoor pony survive when so many other animals died away? It was not easy. Their **habitat** was not very hospitable. The **moors**—areas of open, rolling **wasteland** where the ponies lived—were cold and wet with bitter winds. In addition, humans in the area hunted the ponies for food, greatly reducing their numbers.

But the ponies were very tough and able to survive in areas where few other animals could live. Scientists believe there are several reasons for the Exmoor pony's ability to survive.

One of these is coloration. Exmoor ponies are always brown with lighter "oatmeal-colored" markings around their eyes and on their muzzles. Their manes, tails, and legs are darker than their bodies. This pattern of coloration helps the ponies blend in with their surroundings, making it more difficult for **predators** to see them.

The Exmoor pony's thick coat is another reason it can survive in the harsh climate. The coat grows in two layers. Next to the skin, the hairs are soft and fine. This thick inner coat acts like a blanket, keeping the pony warm in the coldest weather. In the summer, Exmoor ponies shed their inner coats. During warm weather, they do not need this warm "blanket." The outer coat is quite different. Here the hairs are more wiry, coarse, and somewhat greasy. This layer acts as a raincoat. Rain slides easily off this outer coat. When snow falls on the pony's back, the pony simply shakes it off.

The Exmoor pony's teeth have also helped it survive. These ponies have sharp, curved teeth, well-suited for biting through the coarse grasses found on the moors. They also have large molars that enable them to chew these tough plants.

In spite of these natural advantages, the Exmoor pony came very close to extinction. During World War II in the 1940s, the moors where the ponies lived were used for target practice. Some of the ponies were killed, while others were captured and taken to cities to be used for food. This seems cruel, but it is important to remember that many people were near starvation because of the war.

By the time the war ended, only about 50 of the ponies were still alive. The farmers of Exmoor decided to help by keeping and breeding Exmoor ponies. Over the years, the number of ponies slowly began to rise. Today, there are about 1,200 Exmoor ponies. Most of these live on farms. Only about 200 still live on the moors.

In recent years, the Exmoor pony has assumed a role in the **preservation** of the moorland habitat. Some of the plants on the moors are rare and unusual. Nonnative grasses and shrubs, introduced by humans, crowd out these plants, making it difficult for them to grow. The ponies graze on these grasses and eat the tough shrubs that other grazing animals cannot eat. **Conservationists** say the Exmoor pony is doing a good job of helping return the moorland to its natural state. This important job is also helping the ponies because people realize that they are valuable.

The Exmoor Pony Society is a group of breeders who are working to increase the number of Exmoor ponies. They keep careful records of all the Exmoor ponies. In the fall, all the ponies are gathered for branding.

At these gatherings, inspectors examine each foal. Foals with white hair or white patches on their feet are not registered as Exmoor ponies. This is because true Exmoor ponies have no white on their bodies. The society wants to make sure that the breed remains as pure as possible.

When a foal passes inspection, it is branded with a number that is recorded in the society's records. Each registered Exmoor can be identified by these records.

Today, Exmoor ponies are used across Britain for riding, and pulling wagons or buggies. They are very strong horses for their size and can be ridden by adults weighing as much as 200 pounds. As their numbers increase, they are becoming more popular. A few Exmoor ponies have been shipped to Canada and the U.S.

The story of the Exmoor pony is a story of survival. This sturdy little pony has faced many challenges. It has been hunted by man and beast. It has adapted to changes in climate and habitat. It has learned to interact with humans. But in spite of these successes, its numbers remain small enough for it to be considered an **endangered species**.

Of the 1,200 Exmoor ponies in the world today, there is a breeding population of about 500. Every new foal is an important addition to the species. Perhaps, with continued care and protection, the Exmoor pony will roam the moors of Britain for thousands of years to come.

Questions About The Exmoor Pony

Fill in the circle that best answers each question.

1. When did Exmoor ponies first come to Britain?
   - Ⓐ about 100,000 years ago
   - Ⓑ about 10,000 years ago
   - Ⓒ about 1,000 years ago
   - Ⓓ about 100 years ago

2. All Exmoor ponies are ______.
   - Ⓐ red
   - Ⓑ gray
   - Ⓒ black
   - Ⓓ brown

3. Exmoor ponies have ______.
   - Ⓐ one layer of hair
   - Ⓑ six layers of hair
   - Ⓒ two layers of hair
   - Ⓓ three layers of hair

4. How many Exmoor ponies are alive today?
   - Ⓐ about 100
   - Ⓑ about 1,200
   - Ⓒ about five thousand
   - Ⓓ about one million

5. Exmoor ponies help preserve the moorland by ______.
   - Ⓐ grazing on grasses and shrubs that choke out rare plants
   - Ⓑ cutting up the soil with their sharp hooves
   - Ⓒ making tracks in the snow
   - Ⓓ frightening people away

6. Exmoor ponies were almost killed off during ______.
   - Ⓐ World War I
   - Ⓑ World War II
   - Ⓒ the Korean War
   - Ⓓ the Revolutionary War

Write About the Story

Write about how the characteristics of the Exmoor pony have enabled it to survive in the harsh habitat of the moors.

How have humans contributed to the survival of the Exmoor pony?

Choose the Right Word

Many of the words in the article "The Exmoor Pony" are words you might encounter in science. This exercise will help you learn some of these "science" words.

Complete each sentence with a word from the box below. If you need help determining meaning, find the word in the article and read the sentence in which it is found.

Note: One word will be used twice.

1. Many ____________________ of animals are currently on the ____________________ list.
2. To survive, animals must develop ways to avoid ____________________.
3. The ____________________ of an animal's natural ____________________ is vital to its survival.
4. An organization of ____________________ is concerned with the ____________________ of wetlands.
5. The Exmoor pony is a rare example of a ____________________ animal that has survived to present times.
6. Deserts were once considered a ____________________, but now irrigation allows the land to be farmed.
7. Many people enjoy the Exmoor pony and are thankful it did not become ____________________.
8. Exmoor ponies are helping to return the ____________________ to their natural ____________________.

Word Box

prehistoric	extinct	habitat	wasteland	moors
predators	preservation	conservationists	endangered	species

Where Does It Belong?

Place each word from the box under the correct heading.

moor	predators	beast
mammals	plain	channel
conservationists	scientists	inspectors
farmers	Britain	foal

Animals

____

____

____

____

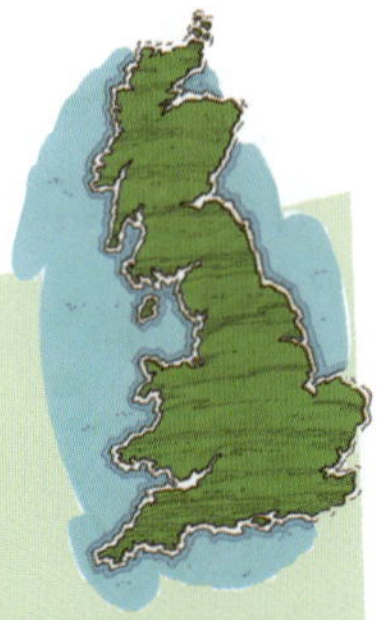

Places

____

____

____

____

People

____

____

____

____

Pre- Means "Before"

In the article, you read that Exmoor ponies are prehistoric horses. The prefix **pre-** means "before." The word **prehistoric** means "before history." It refers to a time before people were keeping records, before any books were being written. It is truly the time before history.

Add the prefix **pre-** to the underlined word in each sentence. Write the new word formed on the line.

1. The baby was born before it was <u>mature</u>. The baby was ____________________.

2. I <u>paid</u> for my book order before I received it. My order was ____________________.

3. The directions said to <u>heat</u> the oven before baking the cake. We had to

   ____________________ the oven.

4. Mrs. Owen wanted to <u>view</u> the film before she showed it to her class. She wanted

   to ____________________ the film.

5. Dad says it is important not to <u>judge</u> people before you get to know them. He tells

   us not to ____________________ anyone.

6. You should use <u>caution</u> to prevent burns when cooking on the stove top. One

   ____________________ is to turn the handles of pots toward the back of the stove so your arm does not knock the pots over.

7. The president's speech was <u>recorded</u> yesterday. Today's news is playing a

   ____________________ version.

8. Clothing manufacturers don't want clothes to <u>shrink</u> when you wash them, so they

   ____________________ the fabric before the clothing is made.

Using Adjectives

The words in the box are adjectives that were used to describe nouns in "The Exmoor Pony" article. Choose an adjective to complete each sentence.

Word Box

natural	tough	rare	hardy
cruel	wiry	endangered	greasy

1. Anita drained the ______________________ french fries on a paper towel.
2. Benji was the little dog whose ______________________ hair stuck out in every direction.
3. Natalie's grandmother has a collection of ______________________ coins.
4. The ______________________ steak was difficult to cut.
5. Mr. Peterson said the rosebush he planted was ______________________ enough to withstand our cold winters.
6. Don't say ______________________ things to your friends.
7. The grizzly bear is an ______________________ species.
8. The ocean is a shark's ______________________ environment.

Find three more adjectives in the article. Write them on the lines.

____

____

____

A ROMAN MYTH

HERCULES

and the MANY-HEADED HYDRA

Hercules is an exciting figure in Roman mythology known for his great strength and bravery. His father was the god Jupiter. Jupiter's wife, Juno, did not like Hercules. When he was a baby, she sent two huge snakes to attack him in his cradle, but the infant Hercules simply took a serpent in each hand and strangled them to death. However, Juno continued to try to harm Hercules. She placed Hercules under the control of his cousin, Eurystheus. Hercules had no choice but to fulfill all of his cousin's commands. Eurystheus required Hercules to perform amazing and seemingly impossible tasks. These tasks are sometimes referred to as the Twelve Labors of Hercules.

This is the story of the second of those tasks.

The land of Argos was suffering. Much of the countryside was covered by a gloomy swamp. A cold gray mist rose from the slimy waters of the swamp, and the **stench** of its poisonous gases fouled the air for miles around. In fact, simply breathing these gases made people sick. No one could venture into the swamp for long without being overcome with nausea. Some poor souls, wandering too near the swamp, were never heard from again.

Now this dreadful mist was not merely swamp gas arising from rotten vegetation. It was actually the noxious breath of a hideous and fearsome monster called the Hydra. The Hydra's body looked like that of a gigantic dog, but its heads—all nine of them—were scaly and reptilian. And all nine of these snakelike heads exuded **dank** and **toxic** mist with every breath, slowly covering the land with a blanket of poisoned air.

Throughout the land of Argos, people whispered and worried about the monster. The Hydra must be killed, they all agreed. But how? Who could venture into that loathsome swamp and come out alive? Who could hope to overcome the powerful creature with nine heads?

Eurystheus, hearing of the situation, commanded Hercules to go and slay the Hydra. So Hercules gathered his weapons—a stout club, a strong bow with dozens of well-made arrows, and a mighty broadsword—and went forth to Argos. At his side was his faithful servant, Iolaus. Together, they made their way directly to the vile swamp. Cautiously skirting the edges of the swamp to avoid breathing too much poison, Hercules and Iolaus looked for the Hydra. It was difficult to see through the thick vegetation and swirling wisps of mist, but at last Iolaus spotted the monster.

"Look, Hercules, there he lies!" whispered Iolaus.

The monster lay beneath the drooping branches of a dark tree some little distance into the murky swamp. The monster's body was curled in a puddle of greasy mud, while its nine heads lay resting on a rotten log. The monster was sound asleep.

"What good fortune!" said Hercules. "We have a moment to plan. But we must be quick, for that monster may soon become aware that we are here. He will awaken from his slumber any moment, and he will be viciously angry."

"Yes," answered Iolaus, "we are surely in peril. What shall we do?"

"Well," responded Hercules, "we cannot attack him as he sleeps. Look at the ground, Iolaus. The Hydra has protected himself well. See, he is surrounded by pools of deep black water that give us no solid ground from which to fight. We must provoke the monster and make him come to us. Here on the higher ground, we will have the advantage."

"Tell me your plan, and my part in it," said Iolaus. "I am ready to fight."

"You are a good and loyal friend," said Hercules, clasping his servant's shoulder. "I am certain that with your help, we will come through to victory. But whatever happens, know that I am grateful for your **steadfastness** and your friendship. Now, move quickly. We must gather wood and build a fire."

The two set about their task with stealth and speed. Soon, a small fire was blazing. Hercules took up his bow and stood at the ready. Iolaus held arrows in the fire until they burst into flame. Then he handed the flaming arrows to Hercules who fitted them to his bow and began to fire at the Hydra. The white-hot tips of the arrows pierced and stung the monster, and he rose up spitting and shrieking at his attacker.

Just as Hercules had expected, the Hydra **lunged** toward him. Hercules took a mighty breath, pulling the air deeply into his lungs. He knew that he must hold this breath as long as possible in order to avoid breathing in the vile breath of the monster. Even though he was blessed with strength and **vigor** beyond that of mere mortals, he realized that he was not completely **immune** to the poison. The toxic breath of the Hydra would weaken him, and he needed every ounce of his power for this fight.

As the Hydra approached, Hercules dropped his bow, picked up his mighty club, and began to swing. With one blow he smashed one of the Hydra's heads, and then another. But to his horror, Hercules saw that his efforts were of no **consequence**. As soon as a head was crushed, two more grew in its place! Tossing aside the club, Hercules drew his sword and began to slash at the heads. But each time he lopped off one of the monster's hissing heads, two heads quickly grew in its place.

Iolaus, seeing the desperation of the situation, took a flaming stick out of the fire and ran to his friend's side. As soon as Hercules sliced off a head, Iolaus laid the flaming branch to the stump of the neck. Once **seared**, the neck could no longer grow a new head.

Hercules slashed and Iolaus burned. Soon the Hydra's heads lay scattered across the swampy ground, and its headless body fell thrashing into the bog. But one of the monster's heads, the center one, could not be killed. Even though the head was severed from the neck, it remained alive and lay hissing and spitting at the hero's feet.

Although they were both exhausted from their efforts, Hercules and Iolaus worked together to lift a large boulder from the ground. They dropped the boulder onto the immortal head with a sickening **thud**, burying it deep in the ground where it could do no further damage.

The people of Argos were overjoyed at this course of events. They poured into the streets to welcome Hercules and to thank him and Iolaus for their courage and daring. There was music and dancing and feasting long into the night. Sometime during the festivities, a sweet cool breeze began to blow across the land. It lifted the last of the bitter fog, and swept it away forever, until the poison fumes of the Hydra became no more than an unpleasant memory.

Skills: Recalling Details; Drawing Conclusions

Questions About HERCULES and the MANY-HEADED HYDRA

Fill in the circle that best answers each question.

1. Hercules was famous in the Roman world for his great ______.
   Ⓐ fear
   Ⓑ wealth
   Ⓒ strength
   Ⓓ weakness

2. When Hercules and Iolaus found the monster, it was ______.
   Ⓐ sleeping
   Ⓑ eating
   Ⓒ crying
   Ⓓ dead

3. When Hercules destroyed one of Hydra's heads, ______.
   Ⓐ another monster came out of the swamp to help the Hydra
   Ⓑ the Hydra stepped on Hercules and crushed him
   Ⓒ Iolaus ran away in fear
   Ⓓ more heads grew in its place

4. Iolaus solved the problem by ______.
   Ⓐ using a flaming stick to sear the Hydra's necks
   Ⓑ using ice to freeze the Hydra's necks
   Ⓒ throwing water on the Hydra
   Ⓓ putting tar on the Hydra

5. Hercules and Iolaus disposed of the Hydra's center head by ______.
   Ⓐ burning it in the fire
   Ⓑ burying it under a rock
   Ⓒ throwing it in the river
   Ⓓ running over it with their chariot

6. Hercules and Iolaus were able to kill the Hydra because ______.
   Ⓐ the Hydra was quite old
   Ⓑ Hercules knew a magic spell
   Ⓒ they were stronger than the Hydra
   Ⓓ they worked together as a team

True or False?

Write a T in front of each statement that is true.
Write an F in front of each statement that is false.

_____ The Hydra had the body of a lizard and the heads of a cat.

_____ The Hydra breathed out poisonous fumes that made people sick.

_____ The Hydra had eleven heads.

_____ Iolaus did not help Hercules kill the monster.

_____ Hercules and Iolaus were good friends.

_____ The people of Argos liked having the Hydra nearby.

_____ Hercules killed the Hydra by shooting it with burning arrows.

_____ A big party was held to celebrate the Hydra's death.

_____ The poison fumes were washed away by a rainstorm.

_____ Hercules wanted to fight the Hydra on solid ground.

Choose the Right Meaning

Find each bolded word in the story and read the sentence in which it is found. Choose the correct meaning for the word.

1. The word **steadfastness** would describe someone who is ______.
   Ⓐ lazy
   Ⓑ loyal
   Ⓒ shaky
   Ⓓ nervous

2. The word **toxic** means ______.
   Ⓐ poisonous
   Ⓑ smelly
   Ⓒ tasty
   Ⓓ ugly

3. The word **vigor** means ______.
   Ⓐ hunger and thirst
   Ⓑ anxiety and worry
   Ⓒ energy and strength
   Ⓓ greed and selfishness

4. The word **immune** means to be able to ______.
   Ⓐ speak
   Ⓑ resist
   Ⓒ write
   Ⓓ fly

5. The word **lunge** means to ______.
   Ⓐ charge toward
   Ⓑ fall back
   Ⓒ slip
   Ⓓ flip

6. A place that is **dank** is ______.
   Ⓐ soft and cozy
   Ⓑ warm and dry
   Ⓒ clean and fresh
   Ⓓ damp and chilly

7. Where might you experience a **stench**?
   Ⓐ in a bakery
   Ⓑ in a florist shop
   Ⓒ at a garbage dump
   Ⓓ at a perfume counter

8. If an action had no **consequence**, it ______.
   Ⓐ won no prize
   Ⓑ had no effect
   Ⓒ could not be repeated
   Ⓓ had never been done before

9. Which of these might you want to **sear**?
   Ⓐ a candle
   Ⓑ a tear in your shirt
   Ⓒ a piece of fruit
   Ⓓ a steak on the grill

10. A **thud** might be made by ______.
    Ⓐ a dinosaur walking
    Ⓑ a ballet dancer on tiptoe
    Ⓒ a leaf landing on the grass
    Ⓓ a window being hit by a baseball

Word Pictures

The story of "Hercules and the Many-Headed Hydra" is full of language that creates vivid pictures in the reader's mind.

Draw to show the pictures these sentences create in your mind.

The white-hot tips of the arrows pierced and stung the monster, and he rose up spitting and shrieking at his attacker.

The Hydra's heads lay scattered across the swampy ground.

Hero or Monster?

Some of the words on this page might be used to describe a **hero**.
Some of the words might be used to describe a **monster**.
Some of the words might describe **both**.

Write each word under the heading or headings where you think it fits.

slimy	loathsome	vile	dreadful	foul	hideous
strong	noxious	fearsome	gigantic	mighty	powerful
scaly	reptilian	brave	steadfast		

Hero	Monster
__________	__________
__________	__________
__________	__________
__________	__________
__________	__________
__________	__________
__________	__________
__________	__________
__________	__________
__________	__________

Think about other words that might be used to describe a hero or a monster. Add at least 3 words of your own to each list.

An Awesome Battle

Write a story about a hero who must fight a monster.
Use some of the words from the previous page to describe your **hero** and your **monster**. Use additional paper if you need to.

About the Author

Harriet Jacobs

Incidents in the Life of a Slave Girl

Harriet Jacobs was born into slavery in North Carolina in 1813. As a child, she had a loving family, and even learned to read and write—an uncommon skill for an enslaved person. When she was 12 years old, she was sold by her owners. For the next few years, she endured much abuse by her new owner and his wife, and she also gave birth to two children.

When she was a young woman, she escaped. She spent nearly seven years hiding out in a small attic in her grandmother's house and in a closet at a friend's house. She also spent several nights hiding in a snake-infested swamp! All that time, she lived in fear of being discovered, but she was able to stay in touch with her children. Her owners were constantly searching for her, however, so she eventually escaped to Philadelphia and then to New York.

When she reached New York, she became a nursemaid for a good family. She met important people in the **abolitionist** movement, including Frederick Douglass, Amy Post, and Lydia Maria Child. Harriet felt that she had a story that needed to be told, a story about slavery. She knew how to write, but she didn't think she could write well enough to tell her story. Child and Post **encouraged** her, however, and she began to put on paper the story of her life as an enslaved person.

Her book was completed in 1858. It took three years to find a publisher for her story, but in 1861, *Incidents in the Life of a Slave Girl* was published under the pseudonym of Linda Brent. The story is the **autobiography** of Harriet Jacobs.

In the chapter "Northward Bound" starting on page 67, the story of her long-awaited journey to freedom is told.

Note: The complete book, Incidents in the Life of a Slave Girl, *can be downloaded as an e-book from the following Web site: http://www.gutenberg.org.*

Harriet Jacobs

Northward Bound

A chapter from *Incidents in the Life of a Slave Girl*

I never could tell how we reached the **wharf**. My brain was all of a whirl, and my limbs **tottered** under me. At an appointed place we met my uncle Phillip, who had started before us on a different route, that he might reach the wharf first, and give us timely warning if there was any danger.

A row-boat was in readiness. As I was about to step in, I felt something pull me gently, and turning round I saw Benny, looking pale and anxious. He whispered in my ear, "I've been peeping into the doctor's window, and he's at home. Good by, mother. Don't cry; I'll come." He hastened away.

I clasped the hand of my good uncle, to whom I owed so much, and of Peter, the brave, generous friend who had volunteered to run such terrible risks to **secure** my safety. To this day I remember how his bright face beamed with joy, when he told me he had discovered a safe method for me to escape.

Yet that intelligent, enterprising, noble-hearted man was a **chattel**! Liable, by the laws of a country that calls itself civilized, to be sold with horses and pigs! We parted in silence. Our hearts were all too full for words!

Swiftly the boat glided over the water. After a while, one of the sailors said, "Don't be down-hearted, madam. We will take you safely to your husband, in-----." At first I could not imagine what he meant; but I had presence of mind to think that it probably referred to something the captain had told him; so I thanked him, and said I hoped we should have pleasant weather.

When I entered the vessel the captain came forward to meet me. He was an elderly man, with a pleasant **countenance**. He showed me to a little box of a cabin, where sat my friend Fanny. She started as if she had seen a **specter**. She gazed on me in utter astonishment, and exclaimed, "Linda, can this be you? or is it your ghost?" When we were locked in each other's arms, my **overwrought** feelings could no longer be restrained.

My sobs reached the ears of the captain, who came and very kindly reminded us, that for his safety, as well as our own, it would be **prudent** for us not to attract any attention. He said that when there was a sail in sight he wished us to keep below; but at other times, he had no objection to our being on deck. He assured us that he would keep a good lookout, and if we acted prudently, he thought we should be in no danger. He had represented us as women going to meet our husbands in-----. We thanked him, and promised to observe carefully all the directions he gave us.

Fanny and I now talked by ourselves, low and quietly, in our little cabin. She told me of the sufferings she had gone through in making her escape, and of her terrors while she was concealed in her mother's house. Above all, she dwelt on the **agony** of separation from all her children on that dreadful auction day. She could scarcely credit me, when I told her of the place where I had passed nearly seven years. "We have the same sorrows," said I.

"No," replied she, "you are going to see your children soon, and there is no hope that I shall ever even hear from mine."

The vessel was soon under way, but we made slow progress. The wind was against us, I should not have cared for this, if we had been out of sight of the town; but until there were miles of water between us and our enemies, we were filled with constant **apprehensions** that the **constables** would come on board. Neither could I feel quite at ease with the captain and his men. I was an entire stranger to that class of people, and I had heard that sailors were rough, and sometimes cruel.

We were so completely in their power, that if they were bad men, our situation would be dreadful. Now that the captain was paid for our passage, might he not be tempted to make more money by giving us up to those who claimed us as property? I was naturally of a confiding **disposition**, but slavery had made me suspicious of every body.

Fanny did not share my distrust of the captain or his men. She said she was afraid at first, but she had been on board three days while the vessel lay in the dock, and nobody had betrayed her, or treated her otherwise than kindly.

The captain soon came to advise us to go on deck for fresh air. His friendly and respectful manner, combined with Fanny's **testimony**, reassured me, and we went with him. He placed us in a comfortable seat, and occasionally entered into conversation. He told us he was a Southerner by birth, and had spent the greater part of his life in the Slave States, and that he had recently lost a brother who traded in slaves. "But," said he, "it is a pitiable and **degrading** business, and I always felt ashamed to acknowledge my brother in connection with it."

As we passed Snaky Swamp, he pointed to it, and said, "There is a slave territory that defies all the laws." I thought of the terrible days I had spent there, and though it was not called **Dismal** Swamp, it made me feel very dismal as I looked at it.

I shall never forget that night. The **balmy** air of spring was so refreshing! And how shall I describe my sensations when we were fairly sailing on Chesapeake Bay? O, the beautiful sunshine! the **exhilarating** breeze! and I could enjoy them without fear or restraint. I had never realized what grand things air and sunlight are till I had been deprived of them.

Ten days after we left land we were approaching Philadelphia. The captain said we should arrive there in the night, but he thought we had better wait till morning, and go on shore in broad daylight, as the best way to avoid suspicion.

I replied, "You know best. But will you stay on board and protect us?"

He saw that I was suspicious, and he said he was sorry, now that he had brought us to the end of our voyage, to find I had so little confidence in him. Ah, if he had ever been a slave he would have known how difficult it was to trust a white man. He assured us that we might sleep through the night without fear; that he would take care we were not left unprotected.

Be it said to the honor of this captain, Southerner as he was, that if Fanny and I had been white ladies, and our passage lawfully engaged, he could not have treated us more respectfully. My intelligent friend, Peter, had rightly estimated the character of the man to whose honor he had intrusted us.

The next morning I was on deck as soon as the day dawned. I called Fanny to see the sun rise, for the first time in our lives, on free soil; for such I then believed it to be. We watched the reddening sky, and saw the great orb come up slowly out of the water, as it seemed. Soon the waves began to sparkle, and every thing caught the beautiful glow.

Before us lay the city of strangers. We looked at each other, and the eyes of both were moistened with tears. We had escaped from slavery, and we supposed ourselves to be safe from the hunters. But we were alone in the world, and we had left dear ties behind us; ties cruelly **sundered** by the demon Slavery.

Questions About
Northward Bound

Fill in the circle that best answers each question.

1. What type of story is this?
   Ⓐ nonfiction
   Ⓑ fiction
   Ⓒ fantasy
   Ⓓ science fiction

2. The person telling this story is ______.
   Ⓐ Fanny
   Ⓑ Benny
   Ⓒ Peter
   Ⓓ Linda

3. What was one of the things Linda feared while on the ship?
   Ⓐ that she would fall overboard and drown
   Ⓑ that the constables would come looking for her
   Ⓒ that she would get a sunburn while walking on the deck
   Ⓓ that she would get seasick from the motion of the ship

4. How did the captain treat Linda and Fanny?
   Ⓐ He was rude and grouchy.
   Ⓑ He was very kind and polite.
   Ⓒ He was critical and demanding.
   Ⓓ He was untrustworthy and planned to turn them in.

5. What was the cause of Fanny's great sorrow?
   Ⓐ She had to leave all of her money behind.
   Ⓑ She would never see her mother again.
   Ⓒ She would never see her home again.
   Ⓓ She would never see her children again.

6. Why do you think the captain was willing to take Linda and Fanny?
   Ⓐ He didn't like Dr. Flint.
   Ⓑ He was paid a lot of money.
   Ⓒ He did not agree with slavery.
   Ⓓ There was a lot of room on the ship.

Writing About Feelings

This is what Linda said about parting from her uncle, her son, and her friend as she escaped to freedom:

"We parted in silence. Our hearts were all too full for words!"

What does Linda mean by this?

____

____

What do you think she would have said if she had been able to speak to her loved ones at that time?

____

____

____

At the end of this chapter, Linda and Fanny arrive in Philadelphia. They must have been filled with many emotions. Fill in the blanks to explain the feelings the women were probably experiencing at this time.

They felt happy because ______________________________.

They felt frightened because ______________________________.

They felt lonely because ______________________________.

They felt angry because ______________________________.

They felt hopeful because ______________________________.

They felt worried because ______________________________.

Choose the Right Meaning

Find each bolded word in the story and read the sentence in which it is found. Choose the correct meaning for the word.

1. A **wharf** is ______.
   Ⓐ a train station
   Ⓑ a walking path
   Ⓒ a landing place for boats
   Ⓓ a road for wagons and carriages

2. A person who **totters** ______.
   Ⓐ glides over the floor as if on skates
   Ⓑ walks in a weak and faltering way
   Ⓒ leaps boldly and enthusiastically
   Ⓓ struts confidently and proudly

3. The word **specter** means ______.
   Ⓐ hero
   Ⓑ ghost
   Ⓒ monster
   Ⓓ soldier

4. A person who is **prudent** is ______.
   Ⓐ wild and undependable
   Ⓑ demanding and harsh
   Ⓒ cautious and careful
   Ⓓ careless and silly

5. Another word for **constable** is ______.
   Ⓐ policeman
   Ⓑ fireman
   Ⓒ doctor
   Ⓓ farmer

6. If something has been **sundered**, it has been ______.
   Ⓐ cut apart
   Ⓑ painted red
   Ⓒ stuck together
   Ⓓ stretched and pulled

7. The captain had a pleasant **countenance**. He had a pleasant ______.
   Ⓐ way of speaking
   Ⓑ manner of dress
   Ⓒ gray hair and beard
   Ⓓ face or expression

8. Fanny was in **agony**. This means she felt ______.
   Ⓐ uncertain
   Ⓑ great pain
   Ⓒ nervous
   Ⓓ reserved

9. **Chattel** means ______.
   Ⓐ small talk
   Ⓑ inexpensive
   Ⓒ to rattle or vibrate
   Ⓓ personal property

10. A **vessel** is ______.
   Ⓐ a canal
   Ⓑ a wagon
   Ⓒ a large boat or ship
   Ⓓ a road or highway

Match the Meaning

Find each bolded word in the story and read the sentence in which it is found. Write the letter of the correct definition on the line in front of each word.

1. ______ overwrought
2. ______ disposition
3. ______ testimony
4. ______ degrading
5. ______ dismal
6. ______ balmy
7. ______ exhilarating
8. ______ incident
9. ______ secure
10. ______ apprehension

a. mild and pleasant
b. safe
c. event; occurrence
d. exciting
e. fear; concern
f. statement; evidence
g. gloomy; miserable
h. tense; wound up
i. humiliating; shameful
j. temperament

Fluency: Reading Accurately

This selection was written over 100 years ago. The tone, style, and word choice reflect that period in history. Because of this, the selection probably seems unfamiliar. You may need to read more carefully than usual.

- Read the passage below from the selection to yourself. Pause after reading each sentence to make sure that you understand and can accurately pronounce all of the words. If there are words you are not sure about, look them up in a dictionary or ask an adult to explain them.
- Read the passage again, this time pausing after each paragraph. Think about what you have read. Make sure that you understand the events and ideas described in each paragraph.
- When you are sure you understand the passage, practice reading it aloud. When you are ready, read the passage to a family member, making sure to read each word accurately. Use phrasing and intonation to help convey meaning.

I never could tell how we reached the wharf. My brain was all of a whirl, and my limbs tottered under me. At an appointed place we met my uncle Phillip, who had started before us on a different route, that he might reach the wharf first, and give us timely warning if there was any danger.

A row-boat was in readiness. As I was about to step in, I felt something pull me gently, and turning round I saw Benny, looking pale and anxious. He whispered in my ear, "I've been peeping into the doctor's window, and he's at home. Good by, mother. Don't cry; I'll come." He hastened away.

I clasped the hand of my good uncle, to whom I owed so much, and of Peter, the brave, generous friend who had volunteered to run such terrible risks to secure my safety. To this day I remember how his bright face beamed with joy, when he told me he had discovered a safe method for me to escape.

Yet that intelligent, enterprising, noble-hearted man was a chattel! Liable, by the laws of a country that calls itself civilized, to be sold with horses and pigs! We parted in silence. Our hearts were all too full for words!

Skills: Critical Thinking; Writing a Personal Narrative

Write About the Story

Use the information presented on the timeline to provide clues to answers for questions 1 and 2.

- **1813** Harriet Jacobs was born into slavery in North Carolina.
- **1838** The Underground Railroad was set up to help enslaved people escape.
- **1842** Harriet Jacobs escaped to Philadelphia.
- **1850** Congress passed the Fugitive Slave Act making it a federal crime to provide aid to a runaway.
- **1853** Harriet Jacobs began writing her story in a series of letters under the pen name of Linda Brent.
- **1861** The American Civil War began; *Incidents in the Life of a Slave Girl* was published.
- **1863** President Lincoln issued the Emancipation Proclamation, which freed all enslaved people held in those states in rebellion against the United States.

1. The following quotation is taken from the chapter you have read:
   Don't be down-hearted, madam. We will take you safely to your husband in----."

   Why do you think the author placed a blank line in the story here?

   ____

   ____

2. Many writers have chosen to use a **pseudonym**. Mark Twain and O'Henry are both pseudonyms. In your own words, tell what a pseudonym is and explain why you believe Harriet Jacobs used one.

   ____

   ____

3. This chapter is taken from an **autobiography**. What is an autobiography and how does it differ from a biography?

   ____

   ____

A Clever Jester Fools a King

Once upon a time, there was a powerful kingdom called Milliplutz. The king who ruled this domain was King Jan. Despite the worldly power he wielded, the king was deeply depressed. The only thing that seemed to relieve the king's gloom was his favorite jester, Matenko. For many years, Matenko served his king faithfully. He was a master at telling jokes, a **genius at mimicry**, and an expert at executing hilarious pratfalls.

As time passed and old age set in, the king slowly began to abandon his misery. He now recognized what great fortune it was to have been born a king. But while the king's condition improved with age, the old jester's grew steadily worse. His voice was so worn by age that his jokes were **inaudible**. And like his voice, his body had aged poorly. Too many times he had thrown himself down upon the hard ground in the hopes of entertaining his king. Now his whole body ached from morning 'til night.

The kingdom had also aged and changed. The king's court had become a bustling center for the important and powerful. Indeed, it had become such a crowded place that the king often retreated to his private **quarters** in search of solitude. In any case, there was no longer room for a **geriatric** jester and his wife.

It was for the purpose of telling him this that the king **summoned** Matenko to his chamber early one morning.

"Matenko, my favorite joker," he began, "you have served me well for all these years."

Matenko stooped down to graciously kiss the hand of the king. Hearing the popping in his joints and seeing the **wince** of pain that crossed his face, the king reached out and restrained his old friend.

"Now, now, none of that," he said to the jester. "I have lived long enough to know that little but fortune separates the king from his servants."

Matenko blushed, not knowing what to say. Although the king had made his fondness for the clown known, he had never before spoken to him in such a way. He merely looked up at the king **sheepishly**.

"It is not an easy thing to tell one's prized fool that the time has come for him to leave," the king began. "But I am afraid you are simply no longer able to make me laugh. Even your greatest efforts, given the poor state of your health, inspire only pity in me."

Matenko looked as though he would cry. True pity for the clown began to wash over the king. He resumed speaking quickly in an effort to keep his emotions composed.

"You see, I have asked for two new jesters, young ones, to be sent from the school. They will room together in your quarters, and you and your wife can move to town. I've purchased a nice cottage for you to live in. Here is the key. Take this as well," the king said, as he handed a small **purse** of gold to Matenko.

The jester thanked the king and then with considerable effort rose to his feet and shuffled down the hall. When Matenko told his wife Elzunia the news, she broke down in tears. The two packed up their belongings and began the long walk down the hill into the village.

They found their new cottage home without much trouble and began to settle in. Life was not so bad for the first few months, but as the purse began to grow empty, so did Matenko and Elzunia's stomachs. The jester's wife was terribly upset by their circumstances and asked Matenko to go ask the king for more money. But Matenko knew that if he did this once, he would have to do it again.

"Going around begging is not the life for us, Elzunia," he told her. "Give me some more time to think of a plan."

Before long, Matenko had his plan. He went and pulled an onion from the cottage garden and cut it in half. Then he called his wife to his side. "Take this onion and rub it on your eyes," he said as he handed her half of the onion. "Then go to the queen and tell her that I have died."

Elzunia did as Matenko directed, knowing that he must have a great plan and being eager to take her part in it. It took her awhile to get up the hill to the castle, but when she did, she found the queen sitting in the courtyard. She ran to the queen and threw herself at her feet. Then she began to wail.

"Oh, my queen. My husband Matenko has died. He took ill last night and this morning was no more."

The queen was distressed by the news. She had always liked Matenko and thought Elzunia a sweet woman.

"Oh, please don't cry," the queen said. "Death is but a part of life."

"Yes," replied Elzunia, "but I am now without husband or money. I am destitute."

"Take this," said the queen, handing Elzunia a purse fat with gold coins. "It should be enough to pay for his burial and keep you well fed and comfortable for many years."

Elzunia thanked the queen **profusely** and made her way down the hill to her husband as quickly as she could. But when she reached their home, he was nowhere to be seen. All that she found was a small note reading, "Off to see the king. Be back soon."

It had taken Matenko even longer to get up the hill than it had taken his wife. At last, he reached the castle and found the king in his chambers. He approached the king with teary eyes.

"Oh, my jester, what is wrong? Has something befallen your wife?" the king asked.

"Yes, I am afraid so," Matenko began. "She became ill last night, and by this morning she was no more."

"Oh heavens," the king sighed, laying a hand on Matenko's shoulder. "Here, take this money. It should be enough to pay for her burial and ensure that you can live out the rest of your days without fear of hunger." The king handed a bulging purse to Matenko, who took it and headed down the hill toward home.

When he reached the cottage, Elzunia was waiting for him. "What happened?" she asked. "Why did you go to see the king when I just told his wife that you were dead?"

"To tell him that you were dead," he replied. "It is just the type of joke that the king has always loved. I would be surprised if he does not show up here tonight to discover the meaning of the day's events."

Indeed, Matenko was right. That night when the king and queen recounted the events of the day to one another, they were stunned to discover that both Elzunia and Matenko seemed to have died on the same day. They were even more puzzled by how each had reported the other dead. It seemed like an impossibility.

"After we finish this meal," the king said, "we will go down to the cottage and see what on Earth this is all about."

While the king and queen puzzled over what had happened, Matenko and Elzunia quickly prepared themselves for their guests. First, they coated themselves in what little flour they had left to make themselves look ghostly. Next, they lit funeral candles and placed them all about the house. Then, they lay themselves down in the middle of the floor, side by side, trying hard not to move. The **absurdity** of the situation made it difficult to refrain from laughing, but when they heard footsteps approaching, they lay still as still could be, letting not even a breath escape their lips.

"But how is it possible!" The queen was in disbelief.

"Poor Matenko, I should never have made him leave," the king said. "These new jesters are dreadful. Even in his old age, Matenko could have told a better joke!"

"Why, thank you, sire," Matenko said as he quickly sat up. "It is not too late to take me back!"

The king was shocked, but when he discovered that it was all a joke, he laughed so hard that he nearly fell to the ground. "Matenko," he said through his laughter, "you truly are a great joker. I will hire you just to teach these young fools how to do their job properly. You will have your old room back and double your pay. Your body may be old and your voice tired, but only your mind could have devised such an entertaining puzzle as this."

Matenko and Elzunia were overjoyed. They happily lived out the rest of their days in the court of King Jan. And Matenko, in his retirement, supervised the training of each and every new jester from that day forward.

Questions About A Clever Jester Fools a King

Fill in the circle that best answers each question.

1. The king sent Matenko away because he thought Matenko ______.
   Ⓐ was too old to be a jester
   Ⓑ was stealing from him
   Ⓒ wanted to leave
   Ⓓ was mean

2. Matenko told his wife to rub an onion on her eyes ______.
   Ⓐ to smooth the wrinkles around her eyes
   Ⓑ so that she would smell good
   Ⓒ so that she would go blind
   Ⓓ to make herself weep

3. Matenko wanted his wife to ______.
   Ⓐ entertain the queen and make her happy
   Ⓑ fool the queen into thinking he was dead
   Ⓒ talk the queen into taking him back
   Ⓓ ask the queen to give her a servant

4. Matenko and Elzunia coated themselves with flour ______.
   Ⓐ so that they would appear to be dead
   Ⓑ to keep mosquitoes from biting them
   Ⓒ to keep themselves warm
   Ⓓ to prevent sunburn

5. The king and queen went to the cottage to ______.
   Ⓐ take Matenko and Elzunia back to the castle for burial
   Ⓑ get their money back from the old jester and his wife
   Ⓒ try to uncover the truth about what was happening
   Ⓓ punish Matenko for playing a trick on them

6. The king thought Matenko's joke was very ______.
   Ⓐ cruel
   Ⓑ funny
   Ⓒ stupid
   Ⓓ dangerous

Write About the Story

1. Is this story fiction or nonfiction?

   ____

   How do you know? Give two reasons to support your answer.

   ____

   ____

   ____

2. Humor was very important to the king in this story. What evidence from the story supports this statement?

   ____

   ____

   ____

3. Why didn't Matenko simply ask the king for more money?

   ____

   ____

   ____

4. How did the king feel about Matenko? Give evidence from the story to support your answer.

   ____

   ____

   ____

Choose the Right Meaning

Find each bolded word in the story and read the sentence in which it is found. Choose the correct meaning for the word.

1. The word **geriatric** means ______.
   Ⓐ old
   Ⓑ alert
   Ⓒ young
   Ⓓ drowsy

2. To **wince** is to make a facial expression that reveals ______.
   Ⓐ exhaustion
   Ⓑ anger
   Ⓒ pain
   Ⓓ joy

3. **Absurdity** means ______.
   Ⓐ being commonplace
   Ⓑ being ridiculous
   Ⓒ sweetness
   Ⓓ cruelness

4. The word **inaudible** means impossible to ______.
   Ⓐ hear
   Ⓑ see
   Ⓒ eat
   Ⓓ smell

5. A **purse** that is bulging is ______.
   Ⓐ made of leather
   Ⓑ stuffed very full
   Ⓒ almost empty
   Ⓓ stolen

6. In this story, the word **quarters** means ______.
   Ⓐ coins
   Ⓑ living space
   Ⓒ cartons of milk
   Ⓓ divided into four pieces

7. Matenko was a "**genius at mimicry**." This means he was good at ______.
   Ⓐ tumbling stunts
   Ⓑ telling a good joke
   Ⓒ acting something out silently
   Ⓓ doing imitations of people

8. If you are **summoned** to the principal's office, that means that you are ______.
   Ⓐ given detention
   Ⓑ asked questions
   Ⓒ called to appear
   Ⓓ sent a telegram

9. How would you look if you looked **sheepishly**?
   Ⓐ shy
   Ⓑ silly
   Ⓒ embarrassed
   Ⓓ fuzzy and woolly

10. The word **profusely** means ______.
    Ⓐ scarcely
    Ⓑ absurdly
    Ⓒ carefully
    Ⓓ abundantly

Word Relationships

An analogy is made up of a pair of words that have a similar relationship. Here are just two of the many types of analogies.

An analogy can show the relationship of antonyms:
open is to **close** as **up** is to **down**

An analogy can show an object–action relationship:
hand is to **write** as **bell** is to **ring**

Complete each analogy.

1. **Full** is to **empty** as **rich** is to ______________________.
2. **Happy** is to **laugh** as **sad** is to ______________________.
3. **Husband** is to **wife** as **king** is to ______________________.
4. **House** is to **castle** as **village** is to ______________________.
5. **Milk** is to **cheese** as **flour** is to ______________________.
6. **Ruby** is to **jewel** as **rose** is to ______________________.
7. **Crown** is to **head** as **shoe** is to ______________________.
8. **Jester** is to **joke** as **singer** is to ______________________.
9. **Brain** is to **think** as **feet** are to ______________________.
10. **Funeral** is to **death** as **wedding** is to ______________________.

Make up some analogies of your own. Ask your family and friends to help.

____

____

____

Something in Common

Read each list of words. What do the words in each list have in common? Create a heading for each list.

happiness
sadness
grief
fear

ruby
diamond
emerald
sapphire

king
queen
jester
servant

gold
silver
iron
copper

castle
house
cottage
hut

table
chair
bed
sofa

walk
shuffle
run
prance

breakfast
lunch
dinner
supper

Write It Another Way

Rewrite each sentence, substituting a different word or phrase for each underlined verb. Use a dictionary if you need help.

1. The king <u>summoned</u> the jester to his chamber.

____

2. The mayor's resignation <u>stunned</u> everyone.

____

3. Roberta <u>supervised</u> the building project.

____

4. We <u>resumed</u> our work as soon as the fire drill ended.

____

5. My brother <u>devised</u> a way to keep the squirrels away from the bird feeder.

____

6. Kelly <u>wielded</u> the bat confidently.

____

The Magic Mirror

A Japanese Folktale

In a time so distant that it is nearly forgotten, a man and his wife lived quietly in the Japanese countryside in a place called Matsuyama. The couple had a little daughter who was the greatest joy of her parents' lives. The little family had a very simple but happy **existence**. They had good food that they raised with their own hands and a small but **sturdy** home. Most importantly, they had each other, and they wanted little more.

It came to pass that the man had business to attend to in the great city. The city was far away and the journey was difficult, so the mother stayed at home with her child. The woman had never traveled more than a few miles away and knew little of the world, and although she was curious, she was content to remain at home. She missed her husband while he was gone and worried about his safety, but for the sake of her daughter, she hid those worries behind songs and smiles.

At last, the happy day arrived when the man returned, his arms full of packages. The little family sat together on the mats of their cottage floor and gazed with wonder at the **array** of beautiful items the man took from his bundles. There was a **delicate** doll for the little girl, some spices and a new cooking pot for the kitchen, and a packet of sewing needles and bright threads. The mother and daughter laughed and **chattered** excitedly over the treasures, while the father told them all about his adventure.

After a while, when the little girl was busy with her new doll, the father brought out a final gift for his wife. It was unlike any object she had ever seen before. It was a round mirror, crafted of silver and decorated with a scene featuring trees, birds, and flowers. When the woman looked into the mirror's shining **surface**, she was amazed.

"Who is this woman?" cried the mother in surprise. "She is so lovely!"

The husband laughed as he explained to his dear wife that the beautiful face she saw in the mirror was her very own. He told her that mirrors were **commonplace** in the city, but that hers was the first in the village. He told her that the mirror was fragile and could easily be broken, so she put it away with great care in a place where it was sure to be safe.

Time passed, and the little family went on with their lives as usual. The little girl grew up to be a most kind and **obedient** daughter, and everyone who saw her **commented** that she looked exactly like her own dear mother. Both father and mother thought their daughter a beautiful young woman, but they never showed her the mirror because they did not want her to become proud and **vain**.

After some years had unfolded in this quiet way, there came a day when **tragedy** visited the little family. The mother became terribly ill. Father and daughter did all in their power, but the **situation** was hopeless. At last, the mother, knowing she was soon to pass from the Earth, called her daughter to her side.

She drew the mirror from its hiding place and put it into her daughter's hands. Then she spoke. "I soon must leave you, my **precious** daughter. But do as I say. Look into this mirror every day and you will see me, loving you and caring for you as always I have done."

The daughter promised, and the mother closed her eyes in peace. Soon after, the good mother died, and the father and daughter buried her with tears and sorrow. Their grief was powerful, for their loss was great.

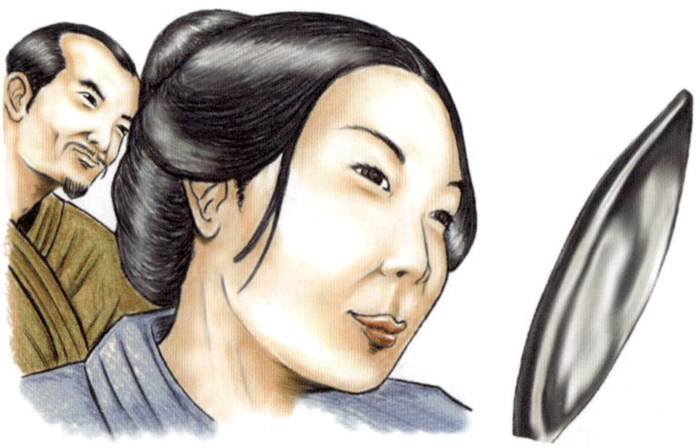

But every day, the daughter looked into the mirror as her mother had directed. And every day, she saw her mother's beautiful face looking out at her and was comforted.

One day, as she was looking into the mirror, her father came into the room. He was surprised to see the mirror, for he had forgotten all about it. "Why, look at that!" he exclaimed. "Your mother must have hidden that away. Where did you find it?"

The daughter told him that the mirror had been her mother's final gift to her. And she explained to him that each day, when she looked into the mirror, she saw her mother's lovely face watching over her.

Now the man knew the girl was simply seeing her own face in the mirror, but of course, he did not tell her the truth. Instead, he **marveled** at the kindness and cleverness of his good wife in giving to their daughter this lasting gift of love and comfort. And he wept tears of gratitude for his own good fortune.

Questions About The Magic Mirror

A Japanese Folktale

Fill in the circle that best answers each question.

1. What might be another good title for this story?
   Ⓐ A Mother's Special Gift
   Ⓑ How Mirrors Came to Be
   Ⓒ Lasting Memories
   Ⓓ A Happy Family

2. The presents the father brought back from the city included ______.
   Ⓐ a bird, a fan, and some fruit
   Ⓑ a dog, a hat, and some cookies
   Ⓒ a doll, a cooking pot, and some spices
   Ⓓ a watermelon, a flute, and some sugar

3. The woman put the mirror away carefully because she ______.
   Ⓐ did not want her neighbors to see it
   Ⓑ wanted to give it to her sister
   Ⓒ didn't want it to get broken
   Ⓓ didn't like it

4. The father and mother did not show the mirror to their daughter when she was young because they ______.
   Ⓐ thought she would show it off to her friends
   Ⓑ wanted her to remain humble
   Ⓒ wanted to keep the mirror for themselves
   Ⓓ thought she would not take care of it

5. When the daughter looked into the mirror, she felt ______.
   Ⓐ sad because she missed her mother
   Ⓑ angry because her mother had died
   Ⓒ comforted because she thought she saw her mother's face
   Ⓓ frightened because she did not understand how a mirror works

6. The daughter was fooled by the image in the mirror because ______.
   Ⓐ the mirror was magic
   Ⓑ her father told her it was her mother
   Ⓒ her mother's portrait was painted on it
   Ⓓ she did not know that she resembled her mother

Write About the Story

1. Why didn't the mother recognize her reflection in the mirror?

2. Why did the mother tell her daughter that if she looked in the mirror she would see her mother's face?

3. Why didn't the father tell his daughter the truth about the mirror?

4. The story is entitled "The Magic Mirror." What was the "magic" of the mirror?

5. At the very end of the story, we learn that the father felt grateful for his good fortune, even though his beloved wife had died. Why was he grateful?

Choose the Right Meaning

Find each bolded word in the story and read the sentence in which it is found. Choose the correct meaning for the word.

1. In this story, the word **existence** means ______.
   Ⓐ fast motion
   Ⓑ way of life
   Ⓒ morning
   Ⓓ breath

2. Another word for **sturdy** is ______.
   Ⓐ feeble
   Ⓑ strong
   Ⓒ weak
   Ⓓ dull

3. To **chatter** is to ______.
   Ⓐ talk excitedly and rapidly
   Ⓑ yell at the top of your lungs
   Ⓒ speak in a slow, calm voice
   Ⓓ walk in a tipsy or unbalanced way

4. A person who is **vain** is ______.
   Ⓐ sorrowful and remorseful
   Ⓑ conceited and stuck-up
   Ⓒ thoughtful and gentle
   Ⓓ cranky and irritable

5. In this story, the word **precious** means ______.
   Ⓐ fun to be around
   Ⓑ worth a lot of money
   Ⓒ dearly and deeply loved
   Ⓓ very creative and talented

6. The word **commented** means about the same as ______.
   Ⓐ sang a song
   Ⓑ wrote a letter
   Ⓒ asked a question
   Ⓓ made a statement

7. A child who is **obedient** ______.
   Ⓐ is independent
   Ⓑ is pleasant and happy
   Ⓒ minds the parents
   Ⓓ argues and whines

8. Which of these could be described as **delicate**?
   Ⓐ a glass figurine
   Ⓑ a baseball bat
   Ⓒ a wool sweater
   Ⓓ a bicycle tire

9. The word **situation** means ______.
   Ⓐ condition
   Ⓑ a bad spot
   Ⓒ trouble
   Ⓓ confusion

10. The word **gratitude** means ______.
   Ⓐ large
   Ⓑ justice
   Ⓒ a gift of money
   Ⓓ appreciation

Write a Definition

Write a short definition of each word. Use a dictionary if you need help. Then write a sentence using each word.

1. **surface:** ______________________

____

____

2. **tragedy:** ______________________

____

____

3. **marvel:** ______________________

____

____

4. **commonplace:** ______________________

____

____

5. **array:** ______________________

____

____

Fluency: Reading with Expression

This gentle story is told mostly by the narrator. Practice this passage from the story and then read it aloud to a friend or family member. For the narration, use a calm voice that conveys the sadness but also the peacefulness of this tale.

After some years had unfolded in this quiet way, there came a day when tragedy visited the little family. The mother became terribly ill. Father and daughter did all in their power, but the situation was hopeless. At last, the mother, knowing she was soon to pass from the Earth, called her daughter to her side.

She drew the mirror from its hiding place and put it into her daughter's hands. Then she spoke. "I soon must leave you, my precious daughter. But do as I say. Look into this mirror every day and you will see me, loving you and caring for you as always I have done."

The daughter promised, and the mother closed her eyes in peace. Soon after, the good mother died, and the father and daughter buried her with tears and sorrow. Their grief was powerful, for their loss was great.

But every day, the daughter looked into the mirror as her mother had directed. And every day, she saw her mother's beautiful face looking out at her and was comforted.

One day, as she was looking into the mirror, her father came into the room. He was surprised to see the mirror, for he had forgotten all about it. "Why, look at that!" he exclaimed. "Your mother must have hidden that away. Where did you find it?"

The daughter told him that the mirror had been her mother's final gift to her. And she explained to him that each day, when she looked into the mirror, she saw her mother's lovely face watching over her.

Now the man knew the girl was simply seeing her own face in the mirror, but of course, he did not tell her the truth. Instead, he marveled at the kindness and cleverness of his good wife in giving to their daughter this lasting gift of love and comfort. And he wept tears of gratitude for his own good fortune.

An Important Object

The **"magic"** mirror was clearly very important to the daughter in this story because of how it made her feel. Write a description of an object that is important to you because of how it makes you feel. Describe how the object looks, what it is used for, and why it is important to you.

Animal Partnerships

A large shaggy bison bull stands on the tall green prairie grasses. As he **grazes**, a small brown bird lands upon his back and begins digging through the thick fur. The bird is searching for pesky insects that live in the bison's coat. This is a cowbird, and for thousands of years the cowbird and the bison have been partners. The bison provides a moving **smorgasbord** for the cowbird. The cowbird provides a pest **extermination** service in return.

This kind of partnership is called **symbiosis**. Symbiosis takes place among all sorts of animals ranging from birds, to fish, to insects, and even to tiny microbes. There are many known examples of symbiosis. Scientists are sure that there are many more which have not yet been discovered.

The Egyptian plover is sometimes called the crocodile bird because of its partnership with the Nile crocodile. The plover, in what appears to be a **foolhardy** act, walks boldly into the crocodile's mouth. Then it picks shreds of meat and small parasites from the crocodile's teeth and gums. The crocodile could easily swallow the plover in a single gulp, but it somehow knows that the bird is helping. Patiently, the croc opens wide to let the little bird pick and poke around its sharp and dangerous teeth. The plover gets a good meal, and the crocodile gets its teeth cleaned!

Perhaps one of the most interesting animal partnerships involves a bird called the greater honey guide. This African bird works together with an animal called the honey badger. The honey badger is a tough little mammal that eats many kinds of food, including eggs, insects, roots, and berries. But its favorite food is honey.

The honey guide also has a favorite food. It loves to eat honeycomb and the small bee larvae that live inside it.

Here is how the partnership between these two animals works. The honey guide flies about searching for bees' nests. When it locates a hive, usually in a tall tree, the honey guide goes looking for a honey badger. The bird flies around the badger's head, shrieking loudly. The honey guide then leads the honey badger to the hive.

The honey badger climbs the tree and rips the hive open to get at the sweet, delicious honey. The bees try to sting the badger, of course, but its thick fur and tough skin protect it from harm. After the badger eats its fill of honey, the honey guide feasts on bee larvae and honeycomb.

Not all animal partnerships involve birds. There are many partnerships between animals that live in the ocean. The brightly colored clownfish, for example, has an interesting relationship with the poisonous sea anemone. The anemone is an invertebrate animal that lives on rocks or reefs in the ocean. The anemone has many **tentacles**, which are covered with stinging cells. When a fish brushes the tentacles, the poison kills the fish. This is how the anemone catches its dinner.

However, the clownfish is able to swim among the deadly tentacles without harm. Scientists believe that a coating of mucus on the clownfish helps the fish to stay safe from the anemone's poison. But why wouldn't the clownfish simply stay away from the anemone?

The clownfish is noted for its striking and beautiful color pattern. Its flashy white and orange stripes make it an easy target for the larger fish that want to eat it. The poisonous tentacles of the anemone provide a good defense for the clownfish. When threatened by a bigger fish, the clownfish darts into the arms of the anemone.

The bigger fish gets stung by the anemone. After the anemone eats its fill, the clownfish eats the scraps and leftovers. In this way, the clownfish provides an additional service, helping to keep the anemone clean.

The hermit crab also joins forces with other undersea creatures. The hermit crab has a soft body that needs protection. The hermit crab **scuttles** about until it finds a hard shell that another animal has abandoned. The crab "tries on" shells until it finds one that fits perfectly. Then, the crab crawls around carrying the shell on its back.

A sea sponge attaches itself to the hermit crab's shell. When the crab catches a meal, the sponge eats the leftovers by filtering small particles of food through its body. In turn, the sponge helps the crab by providing camouflage for the shell. This helps the hermit crab hide from hungry predators.

Amazing partnerships can also be found in the insect world. For instance, ants and aphids help each other to survive. Everyone is familiar with ants. But aphids are less well known, except to gardeners. Aphids are small green mites that feed on plants. They gather on stems and leaves and suck sap from the plants, causing damage. Gardeners do not like aphids, and they use poisons and sprays to kill these insects and keep them away from their plants.

Ants, on the other hand, love aphids. Aphids **secrete** a sugary liquid as waste from the plant sap they eat. Ants like to eat this sweet waste product, called **honeydew**. In exchange for the honeydew, ants provide protection for aphids. They defend the aphids against other insects that want to eat them. Some ants actually build shelters where the aphids hide at night. Others take charge of aphid eggs, storing them beneath the earth through the winter and then bringing them back to the surface in springtime when they are ready to hatch.

The carrion beetle is another insect that has a partner. The carrion beetle feeds on the bodies of dead animals. This sounds rather dreadful, but it is actually a very important job. The carrion beetle is part of nature's clean-up crew.

Other animals and insects also feed on dead animals. Flies compete with carrion beetles for this food source. Both carrion beetles and flies lay their eggs on the animals from which they feed. When the fly eggs hatch, the carrion beetles eat as many of the larvae, or maggots, as they can hold. But the flies keep coming, and the maggots keep hatching. The carrion beetle needs help!

So the carrion beetle brings a partner to the feast. Each carrion beetle carries several tiny mites on its back. The mites have no wings, which makes travel difficult. The carrion beetle provides the mites with transportation. When they arrive at a **carcass**, the mites climb off the carrion beetle's back. They go to work eating fly eggs and maggots. The mites also help by cleaning bacteria off the beetle's body.

Scientists do not fully understand how these animal partnerships **evolved**. Somehow, the hermit crab learned to seek shelter in empty shells. Somehow, the honey guide learned that the honey badger would be an **efficient** partner. Somehow, the plover learned that it could safely enter the mouth of the crocodile. But no one is sure how these animals discovered the benefits of working together. Scientists continue to study animal partners in an effort to unlock the secret of symbiosis.

Questions About
Animal Partnerships

Fill in the circle that best answers each question.

1. The cowbird helps the bison by ______.
   Ⓐ removing excess hair from the bison's coat
   Ⓑ eating insects that live in the bison's coat
   Ⓒ helping the bison find the best grass
   Ⓓ leading the bison to water

2. The clownfish is protected from the anemone's poison by ______.
   Ⓐ its coloration
   Ⓑ a chemical in its stomach
   Ⓒ a coating of mucus on its body
   Ⓓ a tough layer of scales on its body

3. The scientific term for these special animal partnerships is ______.
   Ⓐ biology
   Ⓑ symbiosis
   Ⓒ psychology
   Ⓓ metamorphosis

4. **Honeydew** is a waste product secreted by ______.
   Ⓐ ants
   Ⓑ aphids
   Ⓒ beetles
   Ⓓ butterflies

5. The plover depends on the crocodile for ______.
   Ⓐ food
   Ⓑ water
   Ⓒ protection
   Ⓓ transportation

6. The hermit crab looks for a shell to live in because ______.
   Ⓐ the shell will keep it warm
   Ⓑ the shell makes it more attractive
   Ⓒ there might be food inside the shell
   Ⓓ its body is soft and needs protection

Write About the Story

1. List three animals that depend on their partners to help them get food.

____

____

____

2. Name one animal that depends on its partner for transportation.

____

3. Why does the sea sponge attach itself to the shell of a hermit crab?

____

____

4. How does the honey badger avoid dangerous and painful bee stings?

____

____

Choose the Right Meaning

Find each bolded word in the story and read the sentence in which it is found. Choose the correct meaning for the word.

1. A **smorgasbord** is ______.
   - Ⓐ a large buffet meal
   - Ⓑ a type of insect
   - Ⓒ a kind of wood
   - Ⓓ a bus

2. The word **graze** means to ______.
   - Ⓐ feed on growing grasses
   - Ⓑ wallow in mud
   - Ⓒ drink slowly
   - Ⓓ wander

3. The word **tentacle** means ______.
   - Ⓐ a head
   - Ⓑ a sharp tooth
   - Ⓒ a large stomach
   - Ⓓ a long tube-like body part used for grasping

4. The word **extermination** means ______.
   - Ⓐ cheering up
   - Ⓑ destruction
   - Ⓒ building
   - Ⓓ washing

5. If you act in a **foolhardy** way, you are ______.
   - Ⓐ brave
   - Ⓑ sensible
   - Ⓒ reckless
   - Ⓓ thoughtful

6. The hermit crab **scuttles** about. This means it ______.
   - Ⓐ hides under rocks
   - Ⓑ moves slowly
   - Ⓒ lumbers
   - Ⓓ scurries

7. If you are **efficient**, you ______.
   - Ⓐ are extremely disorganized
   - Ⓑ never finish your work on time
   - Ⓒ waste no time doing the job
   - Ⓓ make a big mess when you work

8. Which of these might have **evolved**?
   - Ⓐ the use of computers
   - Ⓑ the chair you sit it
   - Ⓒ a flash of lightning
   - Ⓓ your lunch

9. Which word might go with **carcass**?
   - Ⓐ flower
   - Ⓑ grazing
   - Ⓒ plant
   - Ⓓ vulture

10. Which of these is <u>not</u> **secreted**?
    - Ⓐ tears
    - Ⓑ saliva
    - Ⓒ hair
    - Ⓓ sweat

Write a Definition

Answer the questions using complete sentences. Use a dictionary if you need help.

1. What does the word **hermit** mean?

   ____

   Why do you think the hermit crab was given its name?

   ____

2. What does the word **carrion** mean?

   ____

   Why do you think the carrion beetle was given its name?

   ____

3. What does the word **invertebrate** mean?

   ____

   Name an animal from the story that is an invertebrate.

   ____

4. What does the word **prairie** mean?

   ____

   Name an animal from the story that lives on the prairie.

   ____

Types of Animals

Write the animal's name from the story under the correct heading. One category will have only two animals. Add a third animal.

ant	aphid	beetle	plover	cowbird	honey guide
bison	crab	sponge	anemone	honey badger	

Bird

____
____
____

Insect

____
____
____

Mammal

____
____
____

Marine Invertebrate

____
____
____

Create two animal headings of your own and list 3 animals under each heading.

____
____
____

____
____
____

Which Spelling Is Correct?

Circle the correct spelling for each word.

appear	apear	appeer
crocadile	crockodile	crocodile
intresting	interesting	ineresting
partical	particle	partacle
actually	acshually	actualy
poyson	poison	poisson
sevral	severel	several
emty	emptty	empty
camouflage	camoflage	cammoflage
farmiliar	familiar	fammiliar

Write sentences using the correct spellings of three words from the above list.

1. ______________________________

2. ______________________________

3. ______________________________

The Sausage

A Story from Sweden

Inside a small **rustic** cottage on an **isolated** woodland path, a woman was busy preparing dinner and singing softly to herself. Her husband, a woodcutter, had not yet come home from his long day's work chopping wood in the forest. But the sun was sinking low in the sky, and a silver **sliver** of moon was curling in the lavender light. Soon, the woman knew she would hear her husband's big boots tramp, tramping up the path. She would hear his booming voice calling out a cheerful greeting. She would hear the rumbling of his empty stomach, eager for some hot, delicious food.

The woman frowned worriedly as she took a small rough loaf of crusty rye bread from the oven and looked in the larder to see what else she could prepare for the evening meal. There was precious little to be found on the bare and dusty shelves. A small shriveled onion, a handful of yellow lentils, a single purple-topped turnip, and two knotty little potatoes were all that remained. The woman sighed as she set these **meager** vegetables to boil in her battered copper soup kettle.

Suddenly, there came a timid knock upon the front door of the little house. "Who on Earth can this be?" wondered the woman aloud. Her curiosity was aroused, for she had no neighbors at all. In fact, there were no other houses for miles in any direction, and travelers seldom passed through their lonely little corner of the forest. Wiping her hands on her raggedy apron, she opened the door to see a peculiar old lady standing on the humble doorstep. The old lady was dressed in unusual clothes that were rich in color and trimmed in silk and fur. There was an exotic look about the lady, and it was **evident** that she had come from some distant and extraordinary place.

"My goodness gracious," said the woman, forgetting her manners in her great surprise. "Who are you? Where did you come from? How did you get here?"

The old lady simply smiled politely at these questions and asked if she might come in.

"Of course," said the woman, "come in and welcome."

"I have come a-borrowing," said the eccentric old lady, as she swirled into the room, giving off a whiff of some unfamiliar spice. "Might you have a loaf of bread you can spare? I find that my travels have left me quite hungry and hollow. Indeed, I am famished."

Now, the woman hated to part with her precious loaf of bread, for she had no more flour to bake another. But the old lady looked weary and drawn, and the woman could not bear to turn her away empty-handed. So she picked up the warm loaf and tucked it into the old lady's arms. The old lady accepted the loaf gratefully and immediately turned to leave.

At the door, she stopped and turned around, a tiny smile playing around her wrinkled lips. "You have been extremely kind to me at great expense to yourself," said the old lady. "I would like to repay you, and this shall be my gift to you. You and your husband shall have three wishes to spend. Whatever you wish for shall be yours. Be wise in your wishes."

And the door closed behind her, leaving the astonished woman alone again in her little house. The woman rushed out on the porch and looked in all directions, but the old lady had vanished, leaving only a **lingering** scent of spice upon the cool evening air.

The woman sat down in her rocker by the fireplace and thought and thought about the three wishes. She thought of all the things she might wish for: a fine fat Jersey cow to give them milk and cream, a large and comfortable house, or a closet full of lovely new dresses.

"Best of all would be an enormous sack of money," thought the woman. "I am so tired of being poor, of **scrimping** and saving and going to bed hungry. But I must wait for my husband to come home. We can decide together."

And so she sat, and rocked, and dreamed until at last her head drooped onto her chest and she dozed happily in the warmth from the fire. After a time, she was awakened by the sound of her husband's boots tramp, tramping up the woodland path. She jumped from her rocking chair and rushed to stir the soup that sat bubbling on the stove. "Oh," said the woman, "I wish I had a fat sausage to cook for my husband, for he deserves a better supper than this thin soup."

All at once, a pan appeared on the stove. In the pan there sizzled a large crisp sausage. At the same moment, the woodcutter swung open the door. "What's this good smell?" he cheerfully demanded. "You are a grand wife to make me such a satisfactory supper!"

At this, the woman threw her apron over her head and wept **inconsolably**. "Husband, I have been terribly foolish," she said. And she told her husband all about the strange old lady and the three wishes. "When I heard you coming up the path," she said, "I couldn't help but think how hungry you'd be. So I wished for a sausage and here it is."

The woodcutter was a gentle man who seldom lost his temper, but when he heard what his wife had to say, he was overcome by fury. "I see why you weep!" he roared. "You have been foolish indeed! You have wasted a precious wish on a grubby, **measly**, ridiculous sausage! Have your brains fallen out of your head, woman? Aargh, I wish that sausage were sticking to the end of your silly nose!"

Of course, no sooner had he spoken the words than he realized his mistake, but it was too late to call them back. And sure enough, the sausage had leapt instantly from the pan and attached itself firmly to the end of his wife's nose.

The woman began to weep in earnest, tugging at the sausage and wailing hysterically at her husband. "Now look what you've done! You call me foolish and then you do this crazy thing? What have you done, husband, what have you done?"

Together they pulled and twisted and yanked and sawed at the sausage, but to no avail. There it was at the end of her nose, and there it apparently would stay. At last, exhausted, they gave up and sat staring at each other in disbelief.

"What shall we do now?" sniffled the woman.

"Well," said the woodcutter, who was feeling extraordinarily sorry about his outburst and his own disastrous wish, "the answer is as plain as the nose—er, sausage—on your face. We have no choice but to use the last wish to set you right again."

This set the woman to sobbing more energetically than before. "I do not want to go through life with this hideous sausage dangling from my face! But I cannot find it in my heart to deprive you of the last wish, husband. Go ahead, make a wish. Wish for anything your heart desires! I can find a way to manage with this dreadful sausage."

And with this, she let loose a new **freshet** of anguished tears. The woodcutter put his arms around his wife. "Good wife," he said, "you are truly unselfish and I love you for it, but I cannot do as you ask."

He stood back and straightened his shoulders. In a firm voice, he exclaimed, "I wish that the sausage was off my wife's nose and back in the pan where it belongs!"

And so, of course, it came to pass, and the two sat down and ate the sausage and thought themselves very lucky to have it and each other.

Questions About The Sausage

A Story from Sweden

Fill in the circle that best answers each question.

1. At the beginning of the story, the woman was worried about her ______.
   Ⓐ husband's clothing
   Ⓑ husband's dinner
   Ⓒ mother's health
   Ⓓ milk cow

2. Who knocked at the door while the woman was making soup?
   Ⓐ a tiny elf
   Ⓑ a lost little boy
   Ⓒ a strange old lady
   Ⓓ a big hearty fellow

3. What did this person ask for?
   Ⓐ something to ride on
   Ⓑ something to wear
   Ⓒ something to drink
   Ⓓ something to eat

4. What did the kind woman give her visitor?
   Ⓐ her last loaf of bread
   Ⓑ her only pair of shoes
   Ⓒ a glass of buttermilk
   Ⓓ a bowl of homemade soup

5. Why did the husband wish the sausage on the end of his wife's nose?
   Ⓐ He was upset because he was hungry and wanted something to eat.
   Ⓑ He was mad because she had wasted a wish on the sausage.
   Ⓒ He was mad at her for giving food to the old lady.
   Ⓓ He had a headache that made him grumpy.

6. Why didn't the wife want to use the last wish to take the sausage off her nose?
   Ⓐ She wanted to wish for a loaf of bread.
   Ⓑ She liked having the sausage on her nose.
   Ⓒ She wanted to wish for a new rocking chair.
   Ⓓ She wanted her husband to wish for something he wanted.

A Lesson to Learn

Traditional stories like this one often have a moral, or a lesson. What lesson do you think this story is trying to teach?

Explain your answer.

Draw a picture to illustrate the moral of the story.

Choose the Right Meaning

Find each bolded word in the story and read the sentence in which it is found. Choose the correct meaning for the word.

1. The word **rustic** means ______.
   - Ⓐ countrified or rural
   - Ⓑ citified or urban
   - Ⓒ expensive
   - Ⓓ cheap

2. The word **isolated** means about the same as ______.
   - Ⓐ located on a good road
   - Ⓑ nearby and familiar
   - Ⓒ lonely and remote
   - Ⓓ next to an airport

3. In this story, the word **sliver** means ______.
   - Ⓐ a tiny slice
   - Ⓑ a big chunk
   - Ⓒ shiny and bright
   - Ⓓ plain and simple

4. The word **freshet** means about the same as ______.
   - Ⓐ handkerchief
   - Ⓑ sausage
   - Ⓒ basket
   - Ⓓ flood

5. The wife was **inconsolable** over her mistake. This means she was so upset that she ______.
   - Ⓐ turned blue in the face
   - Ⓑ got the hiccups
   - Ⓒ passed out
   - Ⓓ could not be comforted in any way

6. The word **evident** means about the same as ______.
   - Ⓐ sorry
   - Ⓑ obvious
   - Ⓒ hidden
   - Ⓓ difficult

7. He was paid a **meager** amount for his service. Meager means ______.
   - Ⓐ sufficient
   - Ⓑ generous
   - Ⓒ plentiful
   - Ⓓ small

8. Winter is **lingering** this year. Lingering means ______.
   - Ⓐ freezing cold
   - Ⓑ leaving
   - Ⓒ remaining
   - Ⓓ mild

9. Which behavior would be **scrimping**?
   - Ⓐ using only a few bits of the sausage
   - Ⓑ giving the sausage to the old woman
   - Ⓒ eating all of the sausage in a few bites
   - Ⓓ cutting the sausage into two large pieces

10. Which word is a synonym for **measly**?
    - Ⓐ ample
    - Ⓑ wormy
    - Ⓒ spotted
    - Ⓓ meager

Which Word Fits?

Complete each sentence using a word from the story.

Word Box

tramp	eccentric	anguish	famished
humble	timid	battered	exotic

1. Being a ________________ sort, the hero did not brag about his brave deeds.
2. The rare spices came from faraway lands and were very ________________.
3. We were quite exhausted after our long ________________ through the woods.
4. The ________________ household furnishings had definitely seen better days.
5. His ________________ behavior earned him the reputation of town character.
6. The stray cat was ________________ and wolfed down the tuna we offered.
7. Maya is generally too ________________ to ask questions of the teacher.
8. The mother's ________________ was great when it seemed that her child was missing.

Correct the Apostrophes

Apostrophes are used in contractions and to show possession.

it's = it is	what's = what is
Fido's chew bone	a bird's nest

Rewrite each sentence leaving out apostrophes that do not belong and adding apostrophes where they are needed.

1. My younger sisters pajama's were covered with flowers'.

____

2. All the dishes' in the cupboard's were broken except for Sharons.

____

3. We hope its going to be a sunny day on Saturday for Heathers picnic.

____

4. The kids' made a big mess in the front yard of the Johnsons house.

____

5. Of all the horse's in the pasture, Wills is the prettiest.

____

6. When Lydia saw Hildas new baby, she asked, "Whats its name?"

____

7. Somebodys suitcases' were left in the trunk of Angelas' car.

____

8. Shes going to be signing her book's at the mall next Tuesday.

____

Making a Story Map

Fill in each section of the story map by writing key words and phrases about each story element in "The Sausage." Using your story map as a guide, tell a friend or family member the story.

Setting

Characters

Major Events

Conclusion

Baba Yaga

A Russian Folktale

Long, long ago, in the time before time, a charming girl named Olga lived all alone with her father in a cozy and sweet little cottage deep in the Russian woods. The girl's mother had died when she was very small. She could remember no other life than the happy one she led with her papa there in the little cottage. Olga's papa was happy, too, but he was lonely. He worried that Olga needed the guidance only a mother could give.

So Olga's papa determined that he should marry again, and this he did. Olga's new mother always acted very kind and **solicitous** of Olga whenever her papa was near. But when Olga's papa went off to the village to work each day, the woman's behavior changed completely. She became rude and hateful to Olga, **chastising** her constantly and treating her with great cruelty.

Now, Olga did not want to worry her papa or make him feel sad, so she tried hard to get along with her new mother. "Surely," thought Olga, "if I am pleasant and obedient, she will learn to love me."

And Olga genuinely tried to win the woman's affection. She did the most difficult chores without complaint. She swallowed the bitter hurt that rose in her throat whenever her stepmother spoke crossly to her, which was often. Things proceeded in this way for quite some time. Then one morning when Olga's papa set off for work, the stepmother turned to Olga with a strange new light in her wicked eyes. Olga could see that the woman was trying to put on a pleasant expression, but the look on her face was more a frightening **grimace** than a comforting smile.

Olga drew back as the woman leaned close and spoke to her in a voice that was meant to sound sweet and kind. "Olga, dear, I want you to go to my sister's house and borrow a needle and thread to sew up a pair of trousers for your beloved papa."

"But there are needle and thread right here," stammered Olga, pointing to the sewing basket that sat open on the table.

"Foolish girl," said the stepmother. Her voice was less friendly now, but she quickly reverted to her former sugary tone. "Ahem, foolish girl," she cooed. "I need a particular kind of needle and a most unusual spool of thread. My sister has them. Go to her now, like the good girl you are."

Olga knew that something was very much **amiss**. She did not trust her stepmother at all, and was certain that she was up to some foul trick. Nonetheless, she had little choice but to obey. "Tell me how to find my way to your sister's house," said Olga, stalling for time. "I don't know where she lives."

The stepmother took Olga to the door of the cottage and pointed down a twisting trail that led deep into the forest. "Take that trail," said the wicked woman. "Walk until the sun is high above you. Then look for a trail to your left. Follow it until you come to my sister's gate. And hurry, for you will have trouble to go and come back before dark. And you know what happens to children who find themselves in the forest after dark! I shudder to think what might happen to you!" As she spoke, she turned away from Olga, but not quickly enough to hide the **menacing** grin that lurked about her lips.

Olga tied her kerchief around her head and thought quickly. "Mother dear, I will gladly go to your sister's house to fetch the needle and thread for you. Only, don't you think I will need to carry some food with me? It is such a long way, and I will need something to eat."

Normally, the cruel woman fed Olga only stale crusts of moldy bread when her papa was away. In order to keep up the **pretense** and further her **vengeful** scheme, she gathered up some better fare. She stuffed a sack with some scraps of meat, a piece of bacon, some cold rolls, and a bit of butter. She thrust the little bundle at Olga.

"Now go," she screeched, forgetting to use her phony voice. "And see that you mind your manners!" Olga turned and began to trot down the forest path. She hurried, even though she was frightened of what she might find at her journey's end. She followed her stepmother's directions, and at last found herself standing outside a rickety gate staring at the oddest hut she had ever seen. The hut, a dark and squatty little structure, was poised on two legs that looked very much like the legs of a gigantic chicken. The hut bobbed and swayed on the chicken legs, but seemed to catch sight of Olga and settled into place.

"How awful," thought Olga, her heart pounding. "This is the hut of Baba Yaga, the bony-legged witch! I don't want to go inside. But if ever I am to see my dear papa again, I must get this over with."

As she tugged at the rusty gate, it let out a squeak that sounded to her ears like a very sad **lament**. Olga opened her bag and took out the bit of butter her stepmother had given her. She rubbed this on the hinges, and the gate swung smoothly open. As she entered the yard, a large and vicious-looking dog came bounding toward her. Quickly, she found the meat scraps and rolls in her bag and tossed them to the beast. He gobbled up the food, then licking his chops, retired to his post under a tree. Slowly, Olga stepped up to the door and knocked. A servant girl not much older than Olga answered. She was roughly dressed in rags and strings, and her hands were red and cracked from labor. The ragged girl was weeping, and her nose was red and raw.

"Here, you poor thing," said Olga, "take my handkerchief to dry your tears." The servant girl took the handkerchief and led Olga into the hut, where an old woman sat in the dim light. This old woman, sister to her very own stepmother, was none other than the fearsome Baba Yaga herself! She sat at her loom weaving and clicking her harsh iron teeth in rhythm with the shuttle. A scrawny black cat sat by her pointed shoes, from which **protruded** sticklike, bone-white ankles.

"Greetings, Auntie, and best wishes from my mother," said Olga. "She has sent me here to borrow a needle and thread from you."

"Very well," said Baba Yaga. "Sit yourself down here at my loom and work at my weaving while I fetch what my sister desires."

Baba Yaga rose and grabbed the arm of the servant girl. "Bring water for a bath and scrub this morsel. Clean her well, for she'll make a fine lunch." Then she went out to the bathhouse to build up the fire. As the servant passed by with her pails, Olga whispered to her, "Please don't be quick with the buckets. Give me a little time to think!"

The servant girl did not reply, but Olga noticed that she went away to the spring with a slow step and took a good long time about returning. In the meantime, Olga sat at the loom, weaving and thinking. Once, Baba Yaga stuck her head in at the window. "Are you still weaving, little niece?"

"Yes, Auntie," Olga answered. "I am weaving just as you told me."

When Baba Yaga had gone again to the bathhouse, Olga sighed. The little cat drew close to her and spoke. "I am so hungry. That horrific old witch never feeds me. Do you have any food you might share with a desperately hungry cat?"

"Oh, poor kitty," cried Olga, forgetting her own plight for the moment. "I'm afraid I have very little. Just one small piece of cold bacon. But here, you shall have it," she said, and she pulled the last morsel of food from the sack. The cat made short work of the bacon, then jumped up onto Olga's chair and whispered in her ear.

"You must leave here, and quickly. Take the towel and the comb that are there on the chair. The servant girl brought them for your bath. Like everything here, they are enchanted. When that evil one comes after you, throw down the towel. It will become a wide and swift river. If that does not stop her, throw down the comb, and it will become a thick and tangled forest. Now go!"

Still Olga hesitated. "But the hateful witch will hear that I have stopped weaving, and she will catch me before I can get away!"

"Oh no," said the cat, "I will take your place at the loom. Make haste! Your very life is in danger!"

So Olga jumped up, grabbed the towel and the comb, and raced out the door of the hut. The cat sat at the loom, using his paws to work the shuttle and keep the loom clicking away.

As Olga ran out into the yard, the ferocious dog jumped up to stop her. Then, recognizing the one who had kindly given him food, he quietly retreated and let her go. The gate, instead of squealing an alarm, rode silently on its newly buttered hinges.

A few minutes after Olga's escape, Baba Yaga again called out, "Little niece, are you weaving?"

And the cat answered, "Yes, Auntie, I am weaving."

But Baba Yaga was not fooled by the cat's voice, and she came at once to the window. Seeing that she had been tricked, she leapt into the room and began to lash out at the cat.

"Why didn't you scratch her eyes out, you dreadful cat?" she screeched.

"Because," hissed the cat, "she gave me bacon, which is more than you have ever done for me."

Baba Yaga turned to the servant girl, who was now cowering in the corner. "You lazy good-for-nothing! Why didn't you get her in that boiling bath?"

"Because," answered the girl, finding some courage. "She gave me a handkerchief, which is more than you have ever done for me."

Baba Yaga stamped her foot in rage. She ran to see if her faithful dog had caught Olga in her flight and torn her to shreds and pieces. But the big dog lay curled under his tree, resting peacefully.

"Useless creature!" Baba Yaga shrieked at him. "Why didn't you rip her limb from limb?"

"Because," growled the dog, "she gave me meat and bread, which is more than you have ever done for me."

In a frenzy now, Baba Yaga flailed and kicked wildly about the yard. She screamed at the gate, "Why didn't you squeak and sound the alarm, you miserable gate?"

"Because," answered the gate, "she oiled my hinges with her little bit of butter, which is more than you have ever done for me."

Baba Yaga's face was purple and green with fury. Hot bile rose into her throat. She jumped into her magic mortar and, pushing with her magic pestle, skidded away through the forest. She would not let Olga escape her clutches. After some time, Olga heard the sound of Baba Yaga's screams and curses echoing through the forest. Quickly, she pulled the towel out of her sack and threw it down behind her. Just as the cat said it would, the towel became a raging **torrent**. Baba Yaga wailed and gnashed her hideous iron teeth in anger. But she was not about to be outdone so easily. She sped back to her hut and gathered her vast herd of oxen. She drove them to the banks of the magic river, where she commanded them to drink. They drank and drank until the river was but a mere **trickle**. Then she crossed over and continued the chase.

Once again, Olga heard the dreaded sound of the witch's cries. Quickly, she pulled the comb out of her sack and threw it down behind her. Just as the cat said it would, the comb became a dense and tangled forest. Now Baba Yaga became a madwoman, swearing and chopping at the trees and briars that blocked her way. But no matter how much she swore, or how rapidly she chopped, she could not penetrate that enchanted forest. At last, weary with **exertion**, she gave up her **futile** efforts and made her way back to her hut.

Meanwhile, Olga arrived at her own little cottage just as dusk was settling upon the forest. She was overjoyed to see her papa walking toward the cottage on his way home from the village. Overwhelmed with relief, she ran to him and threw her arms around him. "Oh, Papa, you cannot believe what has happened this day!" she cried, as she clung to his neck and poured out her story.

As soon as Olga had finished her **harrowing** tale, her papa took up a great gnarled stick. He ran into the house and told his wicked wife never to set foot in his cottage again. She ran blubbering into the dark forest and was never seen or heard from again. No one knows what happened to her.

After several years had passed, a very kind woman came to be the wife of Olga's papa. This woman was in word and deed a good and loving mother to Olga. And the little cottage was filled with joy forever after.

Questions About *Baba Yaga*

Fill in the circle that best answers each question.

1. Which word best describes Olga?
   Ⓐ clever
   Ⓑ stupid
   Ⓒ timid
   Ⓓ lazy

2. What do you think Olga's stepmother hoped would happen when she sent Olga to Baba Yaga's house?
   Ⓐ She hoped Olga would get a needle and thread.
   Ⓑ She hoped Olga would live happily with Baba Yaga.
   Ⓒ She hoped Baba Yaga would do away with Olga.
   Ⓓ She hoped Baba Yaga would give Olga some nice food.

3. Baba Yaga's hut was unusual because it had ______.
   Ⓐ goat legs
   Ⓑ frog legs
   Ⓒ chicken wings
   Ⓓ chicken legs

4. Baba Yaga sent the servant girl to draw water because she wanted to ______.
   Ⓐ be kind to Olga
   Ⓑ cook Olga in boiling water
   Ⓒ help Olga wash her clothes
   Ⓓ get Olga a cool drink after her long walk

5. How did Baba Yaga cope with the enchanted river?
   Ⓐ She froze the river into ice and walked across it.
   Ⓑ She drove her oxen to the river and made them drink it up.
   Ⓒ She put a magic spell on the river that caused it to disappear.
   Ⓓ She used an enormous sponge to soak up all the water in the river.

6. What was the happy ending to this story?
   Ⓐ Olga went away to boarding school.
   Ⓑ Olga found a giant ruby under her pillow.
   Ⓒ Olga and her father moved to a new house.
   Ⓓ Olga got a new stepmother who was kind and loving.

Write About the Story

Answer each question with complete sentences.

1. How did Baba Yaga's animals help Olga? Why did they do so?

2. How did Olga's father feel when he heard what had happened to Olga?

3. What do you think happened to Olga's stepmother in the dark forest?

4. We are told that the new wife was a loving stepmother in "word and deed." What do you think that phrase means?

Choose the Right Meaning

Find each bolded word in the story and read the sentence in which it is found. Choose the correct meaning for the word.

1. The word **chastise** means to ______.
   Ⓐ hug
   Ⓑ scold
   Ⓒ praise
   Ⓓ forgive

2. The word **trickle** means ______.
   Ⓐ a joke
   Ⓑ a flood
   Ⓒ a tiny stream
   Ⓓ a kind of candy

3. The word **exertion** means ______.
   Ⓐ expense
   Ⓑ effort
   Ⓒ ease
   Ⓓ rest

4. If you are **vengeful**, you seek ______.
   Ⓐ help
   Ⓑ riches
   Ⓒ safety
   Ⓓ revenge

5. The stepmother's kindness was **pretense**. She was ______.
   Ⓐ pretending
   Ⓑ lazy
   Ⓒ truthful
   Ⓓ honest

6. The word **harrowing** means ______.
   Ⓐ cold and uncomfortable
   Ⓑ stressful and disturbing
   Ⓒ delightful and exciting
   Ⓓ dull and boring

7. If you thought your efforts were **futile**, you might feel ______.
   Ⓐ happy
   Ⓑ confused
   Ⓒ hopeless
   Ⓓ successful

8. A grin that is **menacing** is ______.
   Ⓐ threatening
   Ⓑ comical
   Ⓒ inviting
   Ⓓ cockeyed

Baba Yaga used an unusual form of transportation to chase Olga. It was a **mortar** and **pestle**. Find out what a **mortar** and **pestle** looks like and draw it here.

Figure Out the Meaning

Use the context of the sentence to figure out the meaning of the **bolded** word. Write the meaning on the line.

1. The once trickling stream became a raging **torrent**.

   Torrent means ______________________________.

2. The staff at the hotel was extremely **solicitous** to our needs.

   Solicitous means ______________________________.

3. Don't be surprised if the children **lament** the loss of their pet for a long time.

   Lament means ______________________________.

4. His expression became a **grimace** when the knife slipped and he cut his finger.

   Grimace means ______________________________.

5. I ran into the table which **protruded** into the hallway.

   Protruded means ______________________________.

6. We could tell that something was **amiss** the moment we entered the room.

   Amiss means ______________________________.

Making a Story Map

Write a brief summary of the beginning, middle, and end of the story in the boxes on the left side. Then use the smaller boxes on the right to record three important details about each part of the story. Write your own response to the story in the bottom box.

Beginning	Detail #1
	Detail #2
	Detail #3

Middle	Detail #1
	Detail #2
	Detail #3

Ending	Detail #1
	Detail #2
	Detail #3

Did you enjoy reading this story? Why or why not?

Fluency: Reading with Intonation

Read this passage from the story aloud. Change your voice for each character. Show the emotions each character is feeling in your voice.

A few minutes after Olga's escape, Baba Yaga again called out, "Little niece, are you weaving?"

And the cat answered, "Yes, Auntie, I am weaving."

But Baba Yaga was not fooled by the cat's voice, and she came at once to the window. Seeing that she had been tricked, she leapt into the room and began to lash out at the cat.

"Why didn't you scratch her eyes out, you dreadful cat?" she screeched.

"Because," hissed the cat, "she gave me bacon, which is more than you have ever done for me."

Baba Yaga turned to the servant girl who was now cowering in the corner. "You lazy good-for-nothing! Why didn't you get her in that boiling bath?"

"Because," answered the girl, finding some courage. "She gave me a handkerchief, which is more than you have ever done for me."

Baba Yaga stamped her foot in rage. She ran to see if her faithful dog had caught Olga in her flight and torn her to shreds and pieces. But the big dog lay curled under his tree, resting peacefully.

"Useless creature!" Baba Yaga shrieked at him. "Why didn't you rip her limb from limb?"

"Because," growled the dog, "she gave me meat and bread, which is more than you have ever done for me."

In a frenzy now, Baba Yaga flailed and kicked wildly about the yard. She screamed at the gate, "Why didn't you squeak and sound the alarm, you miserable gate?"

"Because," answered the gate, "she oiled my hinges with her little bit of butter, which is more than you have ever done for me."

Tracking Form

Topic	Color in each page you complete.					
The Terra-Cotta Warriors: An Army of Clay	7	8	9	10	11	12
The Joy of Camping	17	18	19	20	21	22
Mrs. Groggins	28	29	30	31	32	33
Deborah Sampson, Revolutionary Soldier	39	40	41	42	43	44
The Exmoor Pony	49	50	51	52	53	54
Hercules and the Many-Headed Hydra	60	61	62	63	64	65
Northward Bound	72	73	74	75	76	77
A Clever Jester Fools a King	84	85	86	87	88	89
The Magic Mirror	93	94	95	96	97	98
Animal Partnerships	104	105	106	107	108	109
The Sausage	115	116	117	118	119	120
Baba Yaga	129	130	131	132	133	134

Answer Key

Page 7

Skills: Recalling Details; Making Inferences

Questions About The Terra-Cotta Warriors: An Army of Clay

Fill in the circle that best answers each question.

1. The clay figures were placed in the emperor's ____.
   - Ⓐ barn
   - ● tomb
   - Ⓒ palace
   - Ⓓ garden
2. Why did Emperor Qin order his people to make the statues?
   - Ⓐ They were to be placed all around his palace as decoration for a big party.
   - ● They were to be placed in his tomb to provide for his needs in the afterlife.
   - Ⓒ They were to be part of a museum showing life in China at that time.
   - Ⓓ They were to be given as gifts to his most valued friends.
3. Many of the figures were broken when ____.
   - Ⓐ a great earthquake rocked the building where the figures are now stored
   - Ⓑ the government decided to get rid of the figures
   - ● the wooden roof covering the figures collapsed
   - Ⓓ vandals found and destroyed the figures
4. Archeologists are trying to ____.
   - Ⓐ sell the figures
   - Ⓑ copy the figures
   - Ⓒ destroy the figures
   - ● restore the figures
5. The weapons that were with the statues ____.
   - Ⓐ are still in working condition
   - ● were probably stolen many years ago
   - Ⓒ were broken during the excavation
   - Ⓓ are of no interest to archeologists
6. Tourists can harm the figures by ____.
   - Ⓐ looking at them
   - Ⓑ talking about them
   - Ⓒ reading about them
   - ● touching them or breathing on them

©2005 by Evan-Moor Corp. • Reading • EMC 4534 7

Page 8

Skills: Recalling Details; Making Inferences; Expressing an Opinion

Write About the Story

Answer the questions using complete sentences.

1. What other kinds of figures were found with the soldiers?
   Acrobats, horses and other animals, chariots
2. What do you think is the most interesting fact about these figures?
   Responses will vary, but must cite information found in the article.
3. How would the statues have looked different had you seen them when they were created?
   The statues would have been painted in lifelike colors; the soldiers would have had weapons.
4. Should tourists be allowed to visit these figures? Explain your answer.
   Responses will vary, but should point out the need for minimizing damage to the figures.

8 Reading • EMC 4534 • ©2005 by Evan-Moor Corp.

Page 9

Skills: Understanding Word Meaning

Choose the Right Meaning

Find each bolded word in the story and read the sentence in which it is found. Choose the correct meaning for the word.

1. An **emperor** is similar to ____.
   - ● a king
   - Ⓑ a clown
   - Ⓒ a scientist
   - Ⓓ a carpenter
2. In this story, we learn that **terra cotta** is a kind of ____.
   - Ⓐ oil
   - ● clay
   - Ⓒ paint
   - Ⓓ metal
3. A **warrior** is about the same as ____.
   - Ⓐ a bricklayer
   - Ⓑ a mechanic
   - ● a soldier
   - Ⓓ a painter
4. The word **elaborate** means ____.
   - Ⓐ old and damaged
   - ● fancy and ornate
   - Ⓒ plain and simple
   - Ⓓ brand new
5. A **fragment** is ____.
   - ● a broken piece
   - Ⓑ a whole object
   - Ⓒ a photograph
   - Ⓓ a blueprint
6. Something that is **fragile** is ____.
   - Ⓐ flexible and stretchy
   - Ⓑ heavy and strong
   - Ⓒ sturdy and thick
   - ● easily broken
7. Which of these might you **excavate**?
   - Ⓐ your stamp collection
   - Ⓑ a burning building
   - ● ancient ruins
   - Ⓓ a funny story
8. If a solution to a problem is **effective**, it ____.
   - Ⓐ is obvious
   - Ⓑ is too hard
   - ● works
   - Ⓓ doesn't work
9. The word **regulated** means ____.
   - Ⓐ made easy
   - Ⓑ found out
   - Ⓒ retrained
   - ● controlled
10. Which of these things would be likely to be **restored**?
    - ● an old car
    - Ⓑ a sandwich
    - Ⓒ a broken window
    - Ⓓ a spelling test grade

©2005 by Evan-Moor Corp. • Reading • EMC 4534 9

Page 10

Skills: Using Vocabulary in Context

Which Word Fits?

Complete each sentence using a word from the story.

Word Box: chariots, communication, lavish, counselor, archers, hues, tomb, artifacts, crafted, rank

1. The counselor advised Allan to take algebra and biology.
2. Lacey used bright, vibrant hues to create her painting of the sunset.
3. In Williamsburg, we saw many artifacts from the colonial period.
4. Uncle Bud gave a lavish party to celebrate his daughter's wedding.
5. The tomb of the pharaoh is deep inside the pyramid.
6. Helen bought a lovely basket that was crafted from pine needles.
7. The Romans sometimes used chariots for travel and for racing.
8. E-mail has made communication much easier and more convenient.
9. My grandfather reached the rank of general, the highest in the army.
10. The archers shot their arrows at the oncoming soldiers.

Write your own sentences using two interesting words from the story.

10 Reading • EMC 4534 • ©2005 by Evan-Moor Corp.

Page 11

Skills: Critical Thinking

Fact or Opinion?

A fact tells information that is true.
An opinion tells about someone's thoughts or feelings.

Write fact or opinion after each statement.

1. The terra-cotta warriors are very interesting. opinion
2. Emperor Qin was a good emperor. opinion
3. Thousands of tourists visit the terra-cotta warriors each year. fact
4. The figures include horses and other animals. fact
5. The horses are the most beautiful figures. opinion
6. The statues were once painted in lifelike colors. fact
7. It would be fun to be an archeologist. opinion
8. Bacteria and mold can harm the figures. fact
9. It was silly for the emperor to have these figures made. opinion
10. It is important for people to know about history. opinion

Write one fact and one opinion of your own. Ask a family member to tell which is which.

©2005 by Evan-Moor Corp. • Reading • EMC 4534 11

Page 12

Skills: Identifying Correct Spelling

Which Spelling Is Correct?

Circle the correct spelling for each word.

(individual)	individule	individial
soldere	(soldier)	solldier
(statue)	stachue	stasue
unaform	(uniform)	uneform
expresion	expreshun	(expression)
counsellor	counseler	(counselor)
serias	serrious	(serious)
(energy)	ennergy	energie
axidental	(accidental)	accidenttal
(guarding)	garding	gaurding

Write sentences using the correct spellings of three words from the list.

1.
2.
3.

12 Reading • EMC 4534 • ©2005 by Evan-Moor Corp.

Page 17

Skills: Recalling Details; Sequencing

Questions About The Joy of Camping

Fill in the circle that best answers each question.

1. You should practice setting up your tent ____.
   - Ⓐ after you select your campsite
   - ● before your first camping trip
   - Ⓒ after you gather firewood
   - Ⓓ before you purchase it
2. You should zip up your tent ____.
   - ● after you arrange your sleeping bag
   - Ⓑ before you choose a campsite
   - Ⓒ before you get out of the car
   - Ⓓ after you gather firewood
3. What is the first thing you should do after choosing a campsite?
   - Ⓐ run and play
   - Ⓑ bather firewood
   - Ⓒ eat some snacks
   - ● remove sticks and rocks from the tent area
4. You should only gather firewood after ____.
   - Ⓐ taking a nap in your tent
   - Ⓑ looking to see if a ranger is in the area
   - ● making sure that firewood gathering is allowed
   - Ⓓ checking to see if other campers are gathering wood
5. The last thing you should do before you leave your campsite is ____.
   - Ⓐ take a picture
   - Ⓑ take down your tent
   - Ⓒ roll up your sleeping bag
   - ● make sure your campfire is completely out
6. This article is mostly about ____.
   - Ⓐ cooking outdoors
   - Ⓑ the National Park Service
   - Ⓒ the hiking trails in California
   - ● camping as a great recreational activity

©2005 by Evan-Moor Corp. • Reading • EMC 4534 17

Page 18

Skills: Recalling Details; Categorizing

Making a List

Under each heading, make a list of as many items as you can remember from the article. Don't peek!
When you have finished making your list, reread the article and add items you may have forgotten.

Answers should correspond to information given, to include:

Sleeping Area: tarp, sleeping pads, tent, sleeping bags

Camp Kitchen: stove, utensils, propane, can opener, dishwashing supplies, storage bags/foil pans

Personal Care Area: hand-washing can, toothpaste, soap, toilet paper, towels, first-aid kit

Extras: camp chair, cards, camera, books, sketchbook, colored pencils, flashlight

18 Reading • EMC 4534 • ©2005 by Evan-Moor Corp.

Page 19

Skills: Understanding Word Meaning

Choose the Right Meaning

Find each bolded word in the story and read the sentence in which it is found. Choose the correct meaning for the word.

1. The word **suffice** means ____.
   - ● enough
   - Ⓑ too small
   - Ⓒ attractive
   - Ⓓ uncomfortable
2. The word **gouge** means to ____.
   - Ⓐ weigh or measure
   - Ⓑ laugh or giggle
   - ● dig or scrape
   - Ⓓ pull or tug
3. The word **submerge** means to ____.
   - Ⓐ hide
   - Ⓑ float
   - ● put under water
   - Ⓓ bury in the ground
4. A **pastime** is ____.
   - Ⓐ something that happened in the past
   - ● a hobby or recreational activity
   - Ⓒ something that is late or overdue
   - Ⓓ a task or chore
5. An item that is **essential** is ____.
   - Ⓐ very common
   - Ⓑ just for fun
   - Ⓒ very soft
   - ● necessary
6. A **gust** is ____.
   - ● a sudden blast of wind
   - Ⓑ a constant breeze
   - Ⓒ a gentle puff
   - Ⓓ a rainstorm
7. Which of these is not **biodegradable**?
   - Ⓐ paper
   - Ⓑ banana peel
   - Ⓒ chicken bones
   - ● aluminum pie tin
8. If you have an **abundant** supply, you have ____.
   - Ⓐ a few
   - ● many
   - Ⓒ not enough for all
   - Ⓓ the last of the bunch
9. Something that is **collapsible** is ____.
   - Ⓐ easy to close
   - Ⓑ side by side, or parallel
   - ● able to be broken down or folded up
   - Ⓓ something that works together with something else
10. A **bin** is ____.
    - Ⓐ a bundle
    - Ⓑ a fenced-in area
    - Ⓒ something that has two parts
    - ● a box or receptacle for storing things

©2005 by Evan-Moor Corp. • Reading • EMC 4534 19

Page 20

Skills: Using a Dictionary; Writing a Definition

Definitions

Answers will vary, but should be similar to examples.

Use a dictionary to look up each word taken from the article. Read the dictionary definition. Write the word meaning in your own words.

1. canteen
   a container for carrying water
2. pristine
   clean, not cluttered or polluted
3. prescription
   medicine ordered by a doctor
4. receptacle
   a container or place to put things
5. potable
   drinkable

Draw a picture of these words:

receptacle | canteen

20 Reading • EMC 4534 • ©2005 by Evan-Moor Corp.

Page 21

Skills: Depicting Ideas Graphically

Map It!

Pretend that you are a bird perched on a tree above a campsite like the one described in the article. Draw a map of the campsite from this perspective.

Drawings will vary, but should include a sleeping area, a cooking area, and a personal care area.

©2005 by Evan-Moor Corp. • Reading • EMC 4534 21

Page 22

Skills: Descriptive Writing; Writing an Opinion

The Best Place to Camp

Write a paragraph about the place you would most like to camp. Be sure to fully describe the place and explain why it would be the best camping spot for you. This can be a place that you have already visited or a new place that you would like to explore. It can even be your own backyard!

Responses will vary, but the description should use vivid adjectives and paint a verbal picture.

22 Reading • EMC 4534 • ©2005 by Evan-Moor Corp.

Page 28

Skills: Recalling Details; Drawing Conclusions

Questions About Mrs. Groggins

Fill in the circle that best answers each question.

1. What day was described in the story as "the worst day of the year"?
   - Ⓐ the last day of school
   - ● the first day of school
   - Ⓒ Halloween
   - Ⓓ Valentine's Day
2. What did Mrs. Groggins do when she wanted to get the children's attention?
   - Ⓐ She rang a bell.
   - Ⓑ She lit a firecracker.
   - Ⓒ She turned out the lights.
   - ● She raked her fingernails across the blackboard.
3. What did Mrs. Groggins do while the children were working on their assignment?
   - ● She read a book and ate a banana.
   - Ⓑ She read a magazine and ate a cookie.
   - Ⓒ She read the newspaper and ate a pear.
   - Ⓓ She ate an apple and played a computer game.
4. How did the children feel when it was time for recess?
   - Ⓐ They felt disappointed.
   - Ⓑ They felt too tired to play.
   - ● They felt happy and relieved.
   - Ⓓ They felt confused and did not know what to do.
5. What happened when the children returned from recess?
   - Ⓐ They went quietly back to work.
   - Ⓑ They lined up and went to the library.
   - ● They laughed and talked and misbehaved.
   - Ⓓ They cleaned the classroom from top to bottom.
6. How did you know that Mrs. Groggins felt happy after she wrote her letter of resignation?
   - Ⓐ She shouted, "Hooray!"
   - Ⓑ She whistled a cheery tune.
   - Ⓒ She smiled a little smile.
   - ● She danced up the stairs.

28 Reading • EMC 4534 • ©2005 by Evan-Moor Corp.

Page 29

Skills: Cause and Effect; Character Analysis

Write About the Story

Answers will vary, but should be similar to examples given.

Complete each sentence to explain why certain events happened in the story.

Mrs. Groggins demanded silence from her students because
She could not stand noise.

Mrs. Groggins did not like the looks of her new class because
They looked and behaved like all children and she found that distasteful.

Mrs. Groggins glared meanly at the children because
She wanted them to stay quiet and still.

Mrs. Groggins woke up with her heart pounding because
She had had a horrible dream.

Mrs. Groggins wrote a letter because
She decided to quit her job.

Write as many adjectives as you can think of that describe Mrs. Groggins.

Responses will vary. Possibilities include:
dreadful, hateful, grumpy, maniacal, menacing

©2005 by Evan-Moor Corp. • Reading • EMC 4534 29

Page 30

Skills: Understanding Word Meaning

Colorful Adjectives

The story of Mrs. Groggins is full of wonderfully vivid adjectives that help paint a picture in the reader's mind.

Find the noun that each of the adjectives below describes. Then match the adjective with its meaning by writing the letter on the line. The first one has been done for you.

Adjective	Noun	Letter
1. puckered	mouth	h
2. brittle	nerves	f
3. hysterical	tears	b
4. unendurable	behaviors	g
5. hideous	dream	j
6. maniacal	teacher	i
7. diabolical	expression	a
8. menacing	sound	e
9. ruthless	gaze	c
10. stunned	look	d

a. wicked; cruel
b. unnaturally excited; out of control
c. having no mercy
d. shocked; overwhelmed
e. threatening
f. easily broken
g. unbearable
h. wrinkled; drawn up into folds
i. raving; insane
j. frightful; horrible

30 Reading • EMC 4534 • ©2005 by Evan-Moor Corp.

Page 31

Skills: Understanding Word Meaning

Vivid Verbs

An author makes a story come alive by using vivid verbs to describe the action. For example, think about how much more descriptive it is to say "She witnessed the accident" than to say "She saw the accident."

Read each phrase below from the story. Use context to help you choose the correct meaning for the bolded verb. Write the meaning on the line.

1. …had been **ensconced** in her sixth-grade classroom.
   settled securely
2. …had never **extracted** the least bit of enjoyment from her profession.
   taken out
3. In truth, she **despised** it.
   hated
4. …her voice sent children **cowering** to their seats.
   cringing; shrinking
5. …they **jostled** their way into the classroom.
   elbowing; pushing
6. …her icy glare, **rendered** all the children as silent….
   caused to be
7. Seeing that look **provoked** a feeling of satisfaction….
   brought about; triggered
8. …the smell of the banana **permeated** the overly warm classroom.
   spread through
9. …**lulled** almost to stupefaction from inactivity and boredom.
   quieted; hushed
10. …the pounding of her heart begin to **subside**.
    decrease; become less

spread through | quieted; hushed | cringing; shrinking | hated | taken out | caused to be | settled securely | elbowing; pushing | brought about; triggered | decrease; become less

©2005 by Evan-Moor Corp. • Reading • EMC 4534 31

Page 32

Skills: Critical Thinking

Sense from Nonsense

Change one word in each silly sentence to create a new sentence that makes sense.

1. Liza led the pledge of allegiance to the ~~class~~.
   flag
2. Rod and Jane passed out math ~~spoons~~ to the class.
   tests
3. When the ~~pizza~~ rang for recess, all the children ran outside.
   bell
4. The teacher told the students to ~~destroy~~ each other's papers.
   read
5. At the basketball game, many parents sat in the ~~bathtubs~~ and cheered.
   stands

Create two silly sentences of your own. Ask a friend or family member to change your silly sentences so they make sense.

1.

2.

32 Reading • EMC 4534 • ©2005 by Evan-Moor Corp.

Page 39

Skills: Recalling Details; Making Inferences

Questions About Deborah Sampson, Revolutionary Soldier

Fill in the circle that best answers each question.

1. Why did Deborah have to leave home and go to work?
   - Ⓐ Her mother did not want to take care of her.
   - Ⓑ Both of her parents had died in an accident.
   - ● Her mother could not support the family.
   - Ⓓ Her father wanted her to learn responsibility.
2. How could you tell that Deborah was a determined person?
   - Ⓐ She learned to sew.
   - Ⓑ She learned to work hard.
   - Ⓒ She worked in a tavern.
   - ● She learned to read and write.
3. Why did Deborah go to a neighboring town to enlist in the army?
   - ● She did not want to be recognized.
   - Ⓑ She thought it would be more fun.
   - Ⓒ Her friends were enlisting there.
   - Ⓓ She wanted to take a walk.
4. Why did Deborah go on a lecture tour?
   - ● Her family needed the money.
   - Ⓑ She wanted to become famous.
   - Ⓒ She wanted to make new friends.
   - Ⓓ She wanted to become president.
5. Who helped Deborah obtain a pension for her military service?
   - Ⓐ John Adams
   - ● Paul Revere
   - Ⓒ Thomas Jefferson
   - Ⓓ George Washington
6. Who was Robert Shurtliff?
   - Ⓐ a friend that Deborah met in the army
   - Ⓑ the owner of the tavern where she worked
   - ● the identity Deborah took on when she became a soldier
   - Ⓓ the kindly minister who got Deborah a better place to work

©2005 by Evan-Moor Corp. • Reading • EMC 4534 39

Page 40

Build a Story

Fill in the blanks with a word from the story.

Deborah Sampson went to work when she was only six years old. Her life was very hard. When she grew up, she became a schoolteacher. Sometimes she would spin and weave to make extra money.

Deborah sometimes wished that she had been born a man. She wanted to have the freedom that men enjoyed. She decided that she would pretend to be a man and join the army. She cut her hair and made a suit for herself. She was as good at marching and fighting as any other soldier. Once, she was shot in the leg. She used her knife to remove the musket ball.

When the war was over, Deborah went home and got married. She had three children. She also adopted a little girl. Deborah died at the age of 67.

In 1983, Deborah Sampson became the Official Heroine of the Commonwealth of Massachusetts. Why do you think she was chosen for this honor?

Page 41

Choose the Right Meaning

Find each bolded word in the story and read the sentence in which it is found. Choose the correct meaning for the word.

1. Which activity is an **invalid** most likely to do?
   - ● lie in bed
   - Ⓑ go ice-skating
   - Ⓒ run a marathon
   - Ⓓ swim in the ocean
2. A **pension** is likely to be received by ____.
   - Ⓐ a prisoner
   - ● a retired person
   - Ⓒ a homemaker
   - Ⓓ a student
3. A **widow** is a person ____.
   - Ⓐ who has no home
   - Ⓑ whose friend has died
   - ● whose husband has died
   - Ⓓ who has never been married
4. Which of the following is an **exaggeration**?
   - Ⓐ I learned to shoot a musket.
   - Ⓑ I carried the musket all day.
   - ● I outran the musket shot.
   - Ⓓ I heard a loud musket shot.
5. A **heroine** is ____.
   - ● a woman who is honored for her courage
   - Ⓑ a man who is honored for his courage
   - Ⓒ a beautiful woman
   - Ⓓ a handsome man
6. What do you do if you **make ends meet**?
   - Ⓐ tie the ends of a rope together
   - Ⓑ make a perfect circle with a drawing tool
   - Ⓒ get back to the place you started
   - ● have just enough money to get by
7. Which of these is **out of the ordinary** today?
   - Ⓐ a woman in the army
   - Ⓑ a woman giving speeches
   - ● a woman as president of the United States
   - Ⓓ a woman flying on the space shuttle
8. Which of Deborah's actions was **controversial**?
   - Ⓐ spinning and weaving in a tavern
   - ● serving as a soldier in the army
   - Ⓒ taking care of a feeble invalid
   - Ⓓ adopting a child
9. The word **military** has to do with ____.
   - Ⓐ sermons in church
   - Ⓑ college classes
   - Ⓒ the movement of birds
   - ● the armed forces
10. The word **resented** means ____.
    - ● felt insulted
    - Ⓑ felt eager
    - Ⓒ felt tired
    - Ⓓ felt certain

Page 42

Make a Match

Use a word from the word box to complete each pair of synonyms, or words that mean about the same thing. The bolded words in the items are in the story. The sentence in which you find each word will provide a clue to its meaning.

Word Box

traded, weak, memorial, gun, shy, jealous, speech, leave, fight, adventure

1. **Bashful** means about the same as shy
2. **Skirmish** means about the same as fight
3. **Envious** means about the same as jealous
4. **Swapped** means about the same as traded
5. **Exploit** means about the same as adventure
6. **Monument** means about the same as memorial
7. **Feeble** means about the same as weak
8. **Lecture** means about the same as speech
9. **Abandon** means about the same as leave
10. **Musket** means about the same as gun

Page 43

Fact or Opinion?

A fact tells information that is true.
An opinion tells about someone's thoughts or feelings.

Write fact or opinion after each statement.

1. Deborah Sampson fought in the Revolutionary War. fact
2. Everyone should serve in the military. opinion
3. Deborah was the bravest woman who ever lived. opinion
4. Deborah was one of seven children. fact
5. Deborah went to work when she was a young girl. fact
6. Children should never have to do any work. opinion
7. Deborah became a schoolteacher. fact
8. Deborah knew how to spin and weave. fact
9. It would be fun to learn how to spin and weave. opinion
10. Deborah Sampson is the most important woman in American history. opinion

Write one fact and one opinion of your own. Ask a family member to tell which is which.

Page 44

Reading a Timeline

Read the timeline of Deborah Sampson's life.
Use information in the story to fill in the missing dates.

1760 Deborah is born.	1766 Deborah goes to work.	1776 Declaration of Independence signed.	1778 Deborah becomes a teacher.	1782 Deborah enlists in the army.	1783 Deborah is discharged from the army.	1789 George Washington becomes the first U.S. president.	1802 Deborah begins giving lectures.	1805 Deborah receives a pension.	1827 Deborah dies.

Answer the questions using information from the timeline.

1. How old was Deborah when the Declaration of Independence was signed? 16
2. How old was Deborah when she joined the army? 22
3. Was George Washington sworn in as president before or after Deborah left the army? after
4. Did Deborah work as a schoolteacher before or after she joined the army? before

Page 49

Questions About *The Exmoor Pony*

Fill in the circle that best answers each question.

1. When did Exmoor ponies first come to Britain?
   - ● about 100,000 years ago
   - Ⓑ about 10,000 years ago
   - Ⓒ about 1,000 years ago
   - Ⓓ about 100 years ago
2. All Exmoor ponies are ____.
   - Ⓐ red
   - Ⓑ gray
   - Ⓒ black
   - ● brown
3. Exmoor ponies have ____.
   - Ⓐ one layer of hair
   - Ⓑ six layers of hair
   - ● two layers of hair
   - Ⓓ three layers of hair
4. How many Exmoor ponies are alive today?
   - Ⓐ about 100
   - ● about 1,200
   - Ⓒ about five thousand
   - Ⓓ about one million
5. Exmoor ponies help preserve the moorland by ____.
   - ● grazing on grasses and shrubs that choke out rare plants
   - Ⓑ cutting up the soil with their sharp hooves
   - Ⓒ making tracks in the snow
   - Ⓓ frightening people away
6. Exmoor ponies were almost killed off during ____.
   - Ⓐ World War I
   - ● World War II
   - Ⓒ the Korean War
   - Ⓓ the Revolutionary War

Page 50

Write About the Story

Write about how the characteristics of the Exmoor pony have enabled it to survive in the harsh habitat of the moors.

coloration enables them to blend in with surroundings; thick coat helps it survive in the harsh climate; outer coat repels rain and snow; sharp curved teeth & larger molars suitable for eating tough moor plants

How have humans contributed to the survival of the Exmoor pony?

Farmers of Exmoor kept and bred the ponies. The Exmoor Pony Society works to increase the number of ponies.

Page 51

Choose the Right Word

Many of the words in the article "The Exmoor Pony" are words you might encounter in science. This exercise will help you learn some of these "science" words.

Complete each sentence with a word from the box below. If you need help determining meaning, find the word in the story and read the sentence in which it is found.
Note: One word will be used twice.

1. Many species of animals are currently on the endangered list.
2. To survive, animals must develop ways to avoid predators.
3. The preservation of an animal's natural habitat is vital to its survival.
4. An organization of conservationists is concerned with the preservation of wetlands.
5. The Exmoor pony is a rare example of a prehistoric animal that has survived to present times.
6. Deserts were once considered a wasteland, but now irrigation allows the land to be farmed.
7. Many people enjoy the Exmoor pony and are thankful it did not become extinct.
8. Exmoor ponies are helping to return the moors to their natural habitat.

Word Box

prehistoric, extinct, habitat, wasteland, moors, predators, preservation, conservationists, endangered, species

Page 52

Where Does It Belong?

Place each word from the box under the correct heading.

moor, predators, beast, mammals, plain, channel, conservationists, scientists, inspectors, farmers, Britain, foal

Animals: mammals, predators, beast, foal

Places: moor, plain, Britain, channel

People: conservationists, farmers, scientists, inspectors

Page 53

Skills: Using the Prefix pre-; Understanding Word Meaning

Pre- Means "Before"

In the story, you read that Exmoor ponies are prehistoric horses. The prefix pre- means "before." The word prehistoric means "before history." It refers to a time before people were keeping records, before any books were being written. It is truly the time before history.

Add the prefix pre- to the underlined word in each sentence. Write the new word formed on the line.

1. The baby was born before it was mature. The baby was premature.
2. I paid for my book order before I received it. My order was prepaid.
3. The directions said to heat the oven before baking the cake. We had to preheat the oven.
4. Mrs. Owen wanted to view the film before she showed it to her class. She wanted to preview the film.
5. Dad says it is important not to judge people before you get to know them. He tells us not to prejudge anyone.
6. You should use caution to prevent burns when cooking on the stove top. One precaution is to turn the handles of pots toward the back of the stove so your arm does not knock the pots over.
7. The president's speech was recorded yesterday. Today's news is playing a prerecorded version.
8. Clothing manufacturers don't want clothes to shrink when you wash them, so they preshrink the fabric before the clothing is made.

©2005 by Evan-Moor Corp. • Reading • EMC 4534 53

Page 54

Skills: Understanding Word Meaning; Using Adjectives

Using Adjectives

The words in the box are adjectives that were used to describe nouns in "The Exmoor Pony" story. Choose an adjective to complete each sentence.

Word Box

natural	tough	rare	hardy
cruel	wiry	endangered	greasy

1. Anita drained the greasy french fries on a paper towel.
2. Benji was the little dog whose wiry hair stuck out in every direction.
3. Natalie's grandmother has a collection of rare coins.
4. The tough steak was difficult to cut.
5. Mr. Peterson said the rosebush he planted was hardy enough to withstand our cold winters.
6. Don't say cruel things to your friends.
7. The grizzly bear is an endangered species.
8. The ocean is a shark's natural environment.

Find three more adjectives in the story. Write them on the lines.

54 Reading • EMC 4534 • ©2005 by Evan-Moor Corp.

Page 60

Skills: Recalling Details; Drawing Conclusions

Questions About Hercules and the Many-Headed Hydra

Fill in the circle that best answers each question.

1. Hercules was famous in the Roman world for his great ______
   - Ⓐ fear
   - Ⓑ wealth
   - ● strength
   - Ⓓ weakness
2. When Hercules and Iolaus found the monster, it was ______
   - ● sleeping
   - Ⓑ eating
   - Ⓒ crying
   - Ⓓ dead
3. When Hercules destroyed one of Hydra's heads, ______
   - Ⓐ another monster came out of the swamp to help the Hydra
   - Ⓑ the Hydra stepped on Hercules and crushed him
   - Ⓒ Iolaus ran away in fear
   - ● more heads grew in its place
4. Iolaus solved the problem by ______
   - ● using a flaming stick to sear the Hydra's necks
   - Ⓑ using ice to freeze the Hydra's necks
   - Ⓒ throwing water on the Hydra
   - Ⓓ putting tar on the Hydra
5. Hercules and Iolaus disposed of the Hydra's center head by ______
   - Ⓐ burning it in the fire
   - ● burying it under a rock
   - Ⓒ throwing it in the river
   - Ⓓ running over it with their chariot
6. Hercules and Iolaus were able to kill the Hydra because ______
   - Ⓐ the Hydra was quite old
   - Ⓑ Hercules knew a magic spell
   - Ⓒ they were stronger than the Hydra
   - ● they worked together as a team

60 Reading • EMC 4534 • ©2005 by Evan-Moor Corp.

Page 61

Skills: Recalling Details

True or False?

Write a T in front of each statement that is true.
Write an F in front of each statement that is false.

F The Hydra had the body of a lizard and the heads of a cat.
T The Hydra breathed out poisonous fumes that made people sick.
F The Hydra had eleven heads.
F Iolaus did not help Hercules kill the monster.
T Hercules and Iolaus were good friends.
F The people of Argos liked having the Hydra nearby.
F Hercules killed the Hydra by shooting it with burning arrows.
T A big party was held to celebrate the Hydra's death.
F The poison fumes were washed away by a rainstorm.
T Hercules wanted to fight the Hydra on solid ground.

©2005 by Evan-Moor Corp. • Reading • EMC 4534 61

Page 62

Skills: Understanding Word Meaning

Choose the Right Meaning

Find each bolded word in the story and read the sentence in which it is found. Choose the correct meaning for the word.

1. The word **steadfastness** would describe someone who is ______
   - Ⓐ lazy
   - ● loyal
   - Ⓒ shaky
   - Ⓓ nervous
2. The word **toxic** means ______
   - ● poisonous
   - Ⓑ smelly
   - Ⓒ tasty
   - Ⓓ ugly
3. The word **vigor** means ______
   - Ⓐ hunger and thirst
   - Ⓑ anxiety and worry
   - ● energy and strength
   - Ⓓ greed and selfishness
4. The word **immune** means to be able to ______
   - Ⓐ speak
   - ● resist
   - Ⓒ write
   - Ⓓ fly
5. The word **lunge** means to ______
   - ● charge toward
   - Ⓑ fall back
   - Ⓒ slip
   - Ⓓ flip
6. A place that is **dank** is ______
   - Ⓐ soft and cozy
   - Ⓑ warm and dry
   - Ⓒ clean and fresh
   - ● damp and chilly
7. Where might you experience a **stench**?
   - Ⓐ in a bakery
   - Ⓑ in a florist shop
   - ● at a garbage dump
   - Ⓓ at a perfume counter
8. If an action had no **consequence**, it ______
   - Ⓐ won no prize
   - ● had no effect
   - Ⓒ could not be repeated
   - Ⓓ had never been done before
9. Which of these might you want to **sear**?
   - Ⓐ a candle
   - Ⓑ a tear in your shirt
   - Ⓒ a piece of fruit
   - ● a steak on the grill
10. A **thud** might be made by ______
    - ● a dinosaur walking
    - Ⓑ a ballet dancer on tiptoe
    - Ⓒ a leaf landing on the grass
    - Ⓓ a window being hit by a baseball

62 Reading • EMC 4534 • ©2005 by Evan-Moor Corp.

Page 63

Skills: Understanding Descriptive Language; Interpreting Information Graphically

Word Pictures

The story of "Hercules and the Many-Headed Hydra" is full of language that creates vivid pictures in the reader's mind.

Draw to show the pictures these sentences create in your mind.

Pictures will vary.

The white-hot tips of the arrows pierced and stung the monster, and he rose up spitting and shrieking at his attacker.

Pictures will vary.

The Hydra's heads lay scattered across the swampy ground.

©2005 by Evan-Moor Corp. • Reading • EMC 4534 63

Page 64

Skills: Critical Thinking; Categorizing

Hero or Monster?

Some of the words on this page might be used to describe a hero. Some of the words might be used to describe a monster. Some of the words might describe both.

Write each word under the heading or headings where you think it fits.

slimy	loathsome	vile	dreadful	foul	hideous
strong	noxious	fearsome	gigantic	mighty	powerful
scaly	reptilian	brave	steadfast		

Hero	Monster
strong	slimy strong
fearsome	scaly fearsome
brave	vile powerful
steadfast	noxious
mighty	reptilian
powerful	loathsome
	dreadful
	gigantic
	foul
	hideous

Think about other words that might be used to describe a hero or a monster. Add at least 3 words of your own to each list.

64 Reading • EMC 4534 • ©2005 by Evan-Moor Corp.

Page 65

Skills: Writing a Creative Story

An Awesome Battle

Write a story about a hero who must fight a monster.
Use some of the words from the previous page to describe your hero and your monster. Use additional paper if you need to.

Stories will vary, but should have a well-developed plot with a beginning, a middle, and an end.

©2005 by Evan-Moor Corp. • Reading • EMC 4534 65

Page 72

Skills: Recalling Details

Questions About Northward Bound

Fill in the circle that best answers each question.

1. What type of story is this?
   - ● nonfiction
   - Ⓑ fiction
   - Ⓒ fantasy
   - Ⓓ science fiction
2. The person telling this story is ______
   - Ⓐ Fanny
   - Ⓑ Benny
   - Ⓒ Peter
   - ● Linda
3. What was one of the things Linda feared while on the ship?
   - Ⓐ that she would fall overboard and drown
   - ● that the constables would come looking for her
   - Ⓒ that she would get a sunburn while walking on the deck
   - Ⓓ that she would get seasick from the motion of the ship
4. How did the captain treat Linda and Fanny?
   - Ⓐ He was rude and grouchy.
   - ● He was very kind and polite.
   - Ⓒ He was critical and demanding.
   - Ⓓ He was untrustworthy and planned to turn them in.
5. What was the cause of Fanny's great sorrow?
   - Ⓐ She had to leave all of her money behind.
   - Ⓑ She would never see her mother again.
   - Ⓒ She would never see her home again.
   - ● She would never see her children again.
6. Why do you think the captain was willing to take Linda and Fanny?
   - Ⓐ He didn't like Dr. Flint.
   - Ⓑ He was paid a lot of money.
   - ● He did not agree with slavery.
   - Ⓓ There was a lot of room on the ship.

72 Reading • EMC 4534 • ©2005 by Evan-Moor Corp.

Page 73

Skills: Making Inferences; Critical Thinking; Character Analysis

Writing About Feelings

Responses will vary.

This is what Linda said about parting from her uncle, her son, and her friend as she escaped to freedom:

"We parted in silence. Our hearts were all too full for words!"

What does Linda mean by this?

She means that everyone was feeling too emotional to speak.

What do you think she would have said if she had been able to speak to her loved ones at that time?

Accept any reasonable, well-thought-out response.

At the end of this chapter, Linda and Fanny arrive in Philadelphia. They must have been filled with many emotions. Fill in the blanks to explain the feelings the women were probably experiencing at this time.

They felt happy because they were no longer slaves.

They felt frightened because everything was new and unknown.

They felt lonely because they had left family behind.

They felt angry because slavery had caused them to suffer.

They felt hopeful because they could make new lives as free people.

They felt worried because they might be hunted; they didn't know what would happen next.

©2005 by Evan-Moor Corp. • Reading • EMC 4534 — 73

Page 74

Skills: Understanding Word Meaning

Choose the Right Meaning

Find each bolded word in the story and read the sentence in which it is found. Choose the correct meaning for the word.

1. A **wharf** is ____
   - Ⓐ a train station
   - Ⓑ a walking path
   - ● a landing place for boats
   - Ⓓ a road for wagons and carriages
2. A person who **totters** ____
   - Ⓐ glides over the floor as if on skates
   - ● walks in a weak and faltering way
   - Ⓒ leaps boldly and enthusiastically
   - Ⓓ struts confidently and proudly
3. The word **specter** means ____
   - Ⓐ hero
   - ● ghost
   - Ⓒ monster
   - Ⓓ soldier
4. A person who is **prudent** is ____
   - Ⓐ wild and undependable
   - Ⓑ demanding and harsh
   - ● cautious and careful
   - Ⓓ careless and silly
5. Another word for **constable** is ____
   - ● policeman
   - Ⓑ fireman
   - Ⓒ doctor
   - Ⓓ farmer
6. If something has been **sundered**, it has been ____
   - ● cut apart
   - Ⓑ painted red
   - Ⓒ stuck together
   - Ⓓ stretched and pulled
7. The captain had a pleasant **countenance**. He had a pleasant ____
   - Ⓐ way of speaking
   - Ⓑ manner of dress
   - Ⓒ gray hair and beard
   - ● face or expression
8. Fanny was in **agony**. This means she felt ____
   - Ⓐ uncertain
   - ● great pain
   - Ⓒ nervous
   - Ⓓ reserved
9. **Chattel** means ____
   - Ⓐ small talk
   - Ⓑ inexpensive
   - Ⓒ to rattle or vibrate
   - ● personal property
10. A **vessel** is ____
    - Ⓐ a canal
    - Ⓑ a wagon
    - ● a large boat or ship
    - Ⓓ a road or highway

74 — Reading • EMC 4534 • ©2005 by Evan-Moor Corp.

Page 75

Skills: Understanding Word Meaning

Match the Meaning

Find each bolded word in the story and read the sentence in which it is found. Write the letter of the correct definition on the line in front of each word.

1. h overwrought
2. j disposition
3. f testimony
4. i degrading
5. g dismal
6. a balmy
7. d exhilarating
8. c incident
9. b secure
10. e apprehension

a. mild and pleasant
b. safe
c. event; occurrence
d. exciting
e. fear; concern
f. statement; evidence
g. gloomy; miserable
h. tense; wound up
i. humiliating; shameful
j. temperament

©2005 by Evan-Moor Corp. • Reading • EMC 4534 — 75

Page 84

Skills: Recalling Details; Drawing Conclusions

Questions About A Clever Jester Fools a King

Fill in the circle that best answers each question.

1. The king sent Matenko away because he thought Matenko ____
   - ● was too old to be a jester
   - Ⓑ was stealing from him
   - Ⓒ wanted to leave
   - Ⓓ was mean
2. Matenko told his wife to rub an onion on her eyes ____
   - Ⓐ to smooth the wrinkles around her eyes
   - Ⓑ so that she would smell good
   - Ⓒ so that she would go blind
   - ● to make herself weep
3. Matenko wanted his wife to ____
   - Ⓐ entertain the queen and make her happy
   - ● fool the queen into thinking he was dead
   - Ⓒ talk the queen into taking him back
   - Ⓓ ask the queen to give her a servant
4. Matenko and Elzunia coated themselves with flour ____
   - ● so that they would appear to be dead
   - Ⓑ to keep mosquitoes from biting them
   - Ⓒ to keep themselves warm
   - Ⓓ to prevent sunburn
5. The king and queen went to the cottage to ____
   - Ⓐ take Matenko and Elzunia back to the castle for burial
   - Ⓑ get their money back from the old jester and his wife
   - ● try to uncover the truth about what was happening
   - Ⓓ punish Matenko for playing a trick on them
6. The king thought Matenko's joke was very ____
   - Ⓐ cruel
   - ● funny
   - Ⓒ stupid
   - Ⓓ dangerous

84 — Reading • EMC 4534 • ©2005 by Evan-Moor Corp.

Page 85

Skills: Critical Thinking; Supporting an Opinion with Facts

Write About the Story

1. Is this story fiction or non fiction?

   fiction

   How do you know? Give two reasons to support your answer.

   Answers will vary, but may mention made up kingdom of Milliplutz; no evidence that people & events were actual.

2. Humor was very important to the king in this story. What evidence from the story supports this statement?

   Answers will vary, but may mention that jester relieved his depression; he hired the old jester back because he was the best jokester.

3. Why didn't Matenko simply ask the king for more money?

   He knew that the money would once again run out and he would keep having to ask for more.

4. How did the king feel about Matenko? Give evidence from the story to support your answer.

   Answers will vary, but should support the idea that the king loved and respected Matenko. He saw to the jester's welfare, even when Matenko was too old to work.

©2005 by Evan-Moor Corp. • Reading • EMC 4534 — 85

Page 86

Skills: Understanding Word Meaning

Choose the Right Meaning

Find each bolded word in the story and read the sentence in which it is found. Choose the correct meaning for the word.

1. The word **geriatric** means ____
   - ● old
   - Ⓑ alert
   - Ⓒ young
   - Ⓓ drowsy
2. To **wince** is to make a facial expression that reveals ____
   - Ⓐ exhaustion
   - Ⓑ anger
   - ● pain
   - Ⓓ joy
3. **Absurdity** means ____
   - Ⓐ being commonplace
   - ● being ridiculous
   - Ⓒ sweetness
   - Ⓓ cruelness
4. The word **inaudible** means impossible to ____
   - ● hear
   - Ⓑ see
   - Ⓒ eat
   - Ⓓ smell
5. A **purse** that is bulging is ____
   - Ⓐ made of leather
   - ● stuffed very full
   - Ⓒ almost empty
   - Ⓓ stolen
6. In this story, the word **quarters** means ____
   - Ⓐ coins
   - ● living space
   - Ⓒ cartons of milk
   - Ⓓ divided into four pieces
7. Matenko was a "**genius at mimicry**." This means he was good at ____
   - Ⓐ tumbling stunts
   - Ⓑ telling a good joke
   - Ⓒ acting something out silently
   - ● doing imitations of people
8. If you are **summoned** to the principal's office, that means that you are ____
   - Ⓐ given detention
   - Ⓑ asked questions
   - ● called to appear
   - Ⓓ sent a telegram
9. How would you look if you looked **sheepishly**?
   - ● shy
   - Ⓑ silly
   - Ⓒ embarrassed
   - Ⓓ fuzzy and woolly
10. The word **profusely** means ____
    - Ⓐ scarcely
    - Ⓑ absurdly
    - Ⓒ carefully
    - ● abundantly

86 — Reading • EMC 4534 • ©2005 by Evan-Moor Corp.

Page 87

Skills: Creating Analogies

Word Relationships

An analogy is made up of a pair of words that have a similar relationship. Here are just two of the many types of analogies.

An analogy can show the relationship of antonyms: open is to close as up is to down

An analogy can show an object–action relationship: hand is to write as bell is to ring

Complete each analogy.

1. Full is to empty as rich is to poor
2. Happy is to laugh as sad is to cry
3. Husband is to wife as king is to queen
4. House is to castle as village is to city/town
5. Milk is to cheese as flour is to bread
6. Ruby is to jewel as rose is to flower
7. Crown is to head as shoe is to foot
8. Jester is to joke as singer is to song
9. Brain is to think as feet are to walk/run
10. Funeral is to death as wedding is to marry

Make up some analogies of your own. Ask your family and friends to help.

©2005 by Evan-Moor Corp. • Reading • EMC 4534 — 87

Page 88

Skills: Critical Thinking; Categorizing

Something in Common

Read each list of words. What do the words in each list have in common? Create a heading for each list.

emotions	jewels
happiness, sadness, grief, fear	ruby, diamond, emerald, sapphire

people	minerals
king, queen, jester, servant	gold, silver, iron, copper

dwellings	furniture
castle, house, cottage, hut	table, chair, bed, sofa

movements	meals
walk, shuffle, run, prance	breakfast, lunch, dinner, supper

88 — Reading • EMC 4534 • ©2005 by Evan-Moor Corp.

Page 93

Skills: Getting the Main Idea; Recalling Details; Making Inferences

Questions About The Magic Mirror A Japanese Folktale

Fill in the circle that best answers each question.

1. What might be another good title for this story?
   - ● A Mother's Special Gift
   - Ⓑ How Mirrors Came to Be
   - Ⓒ Lasting Memories
   - Ⓓ A Happy Family
2. The presents the father brought back from the city included ____
   - Ⓐ a bird, a fan, and some fruit
   - Ⓑ a dog, a hat, and some cookies
   - ● a doll, a cooking pot, and some spices
   - Ⓓ a watermelon, a flute, and some sugar
3. The woman put the mirror away carefully because she ____
   - Ⓐ did not want her neighbors to see it
   - Ⓑ wanted to give it to her sister
   - ● didn't want it to get broken
   - Ⓓ didn't like it
4. The father and mother did not show the mirror to their daughter when she was young because they ____
   - Ⓐ thought she would show it off to her friends
   - ● wanted her to remain humble
   - Ⓒ wanted to keep the mirror for themselves
   - Ⓓ thought she would not take care of it
5. When the daughter looked into the mirror, she felt ____
   - Ⓐ sad because she missed her mother
   - Ⓑ angry because her mother had died
   - ● comforted because she thought she saw her mother's face
   - Ⓓ frightened because she did not understand how a mirror works
6. The daughter was fooled by the image in the mirror because ____
   - Ⓐ the mirror was magic
   - Ⓑ her father told her it was her mother
   - Ⓒ her mother's portrait was painted on it
   - ● she did not know that she resembled her mother

©2005 by Evan-Moor Corp. • Reading • EMC 4534 — 93

Page 94

Skills: Critical Thinking; Making Inferences

Write About the Story

1. Why didn't the mother recognize her reflection in the mirror?

She had never seen herself in a mirror, so she didn't know what she looked like.

2. Why did the mother tell her daughter that if she looked in the mirror she would see her mother's face?

The mother wanted her daughter to find comfort in thinking that she could still see her mother.

3. Why didn't the father tell his daughter the truth about the mirror?

He wanted his daughter to think that her mother was still near and watching over her.

4. The story is entitled "The Magic Mirror." What was the "magic" of the mirror?

The magic was that the mirror helped to keep alive the memory of a loved one.

5. At the very end of the story, we learn that the father felt grateful for his good fortune, even though his beloved wife had died. Why was he grateful?

He was grateful because his wife had found a way for the daughter to feel how much her mother had loved her.

94 Reading • EMC 4534 • ©2005 by Evan-Moor Corp.

Page 95

Skills: Understanding Word Meaning

Choose the Right Meaning

Find each bolded word in the story and read the sentence in which it is found. Choose the correct meaning for the word.

1. In this story, the word **existence** means ____
   - Ⓐ fast motion
   - ● way of life
   - Ⓒ morning
   - Ⓓ breath
2. Another word for **sturdy** is ____
   - Ⓐ feeble
   - ● strong
   - Ⓒ weak
   - Ⓓ dull
3. To **chatter** is to ____
   - ● talk excitedly and rapidly
   - Ⓑ yell at the top of your lungs
   - Ⓒ speak in a slow, calm voice
   - Ⓓ walk in a tipsy or unbalanced way
4. A person who is **vain** is ____
   - Ⓐ sorrowful and remorseful
   - ● conceited and stuck-up
   - Ⓒ thoughtful and gentle
   - Ⓓ cranky and irritable
5. In this story, the word **precious** means ____
   - Ⓐ fun to be around
   - Ⓑ worth a lot of money
   - ● dearly and deeply loved
   - Ⓓ very creative and talented
6. The word **commented** means about the same as ____
   - Ⓐ sang a song
   - Ⓑ wrote a letter
   - Ⓒ asked a question
   - ● made a statement
7. A child who is **obedient** ____
   - Ⓐ is independent
   - Ⓑ is pleasant and happy
   - ● minds the parents
   - Ⓓ argues and whines
8. Which of these could be described as **delicate**?
   - ● a glass figurine
   - Ⓑ a baseball bat
   - Ⓒ a wool sweater
   - Ⓓ a bicycle tire
9. The word **situation** means ____
   - ● condition
   - Ⓑ a bad spot
   - Ⓒ trouble
   - Ⓓ confusion
10. The word **gratitude** means ____
    - Ⓐ large
    - Ⓑ justice
    - Ⓒ a gift of money
    - ● appreciation

©2005 by Evan-Moor Corp. • Reading • EMC 4534 95

Page 96

Skills: Understanding Word Meaning; Using a Dictionary; Using Vocabulary in Context

Write a Definition

Write a short definition of each word. Use a dictionary if you need help. Then write a sentence using each word.

Sentences will vary.

1. surface: the outside or face of an object.
2. tragedy: a sad or terrible happening
3. marvel: to be astonished, filled with wonder
4. commonplace: ordinary, usual
5. array: a display of things

96 Reading • EMC 4534 • ©2005 by Evan-Moor Corp.

Page 98

Skills: Narrative Writing; Writing a Description

An Important Object

The "magic" mirror was clearly very important to the daughter in this story because of how it made her feel. Write a description of an object that is important to you because of how it makes you feel. Describe how the object looks, what it is used for, and why it is important to you.

Descriptions will vary, but should cover the topics mentioned in the directions.

98 Reading • EMC 4534 • ©2005 by Evan-Moor Corp.

Page 104

Skills: Recalling Details; Drawing Conclusions

Questions About Animal Partnerships

Fill in the circle that best answers each question.

1. The cowbird helps the bison by ____
   - Ⓐ removing excess hair from the bison's coat
   - ● eating insects that live in the bison's coat
   - Ⓒ helping the bison find the best grass
   - Ⓓ leading the bison to water
2. The clownfish is protected from the anemone's poison by ____
   - Ⓐ its coloration
   - Ⓑ a chemical in its stomach
   - ● a coating of mucus on its body
   - Ⓓ a tough layer of scales on its body
3. The scientific term for these special animal partnerships is ____
   - Ⓐ biology
   - ● symbiosis
   - Ⓒ psychology
   - Ⓓ metamorphosis
4. **Honeydew** is a waste product secreted by ____
   - Ⓐ ants
   - ● aphids
   - Ⓒ beetles
   - Ⓓ butterflies
5. The plover depends on the crocodile for ____
   - ● food
   - Ⓑ water
   - Ⓒ protection
   - Ⓓ transportation
6. The hermit crab looks for a shell to live in because ____
   - Ⓐ the shell will keep it warm
   - Ⓑ the shell makes it more attractive
   - Ⓒ there might be food inside the shell
   - ● its body is soft and needs protection

104 Reading • EMC 4534 • ©2005 by Evan-Moor Corp.

Page 105

Skills: Recalling Details; Drawing Conclusions

Write About the Story

1. List three animals that depend on their partners to help them get food.

clownfish
cowbirds
honey guide

2. Name one animal that depends on its partner for transportation.

mites

3. Why does the sea sponge attach itself to the shell of a hermit crab?

It eats the crab's leftover food and in turn the crab provides protection for it.

4. How does the honey badger avoid dangerous and painful bee stings?

It is protected by its thick hair and tough skin.

©2005 by Evan-Moor Corp. • Reading • EMC 4534 105

Page 106

Skills: Understanding Word Meaning; Making Inferences

Choose the Right Meaning

Find each bolded word in the story and read the sentence in which it is found. Choose the correct meaning for the word.

1. A **smorgasbord** is ____
   - ● a large buffet meal
   - Ⓑ a type of insect
   - Ⓒ a kind of wood
   - Ⓓ a bus
2. The word **graze** means to ____
   - ● feed on growing grasses
   - Ⓑ wallow in mud
   - Ⓒ drink slowly
   - Ⓓ wander
3. The word **tentacle** means ____
   - Ⓐ a head
   - Ⓑ a sharp tooth
   - Ⓒ a large stomach
   - ● a long tube-like body part used for grasping
4. The word **extermination** means ____
   - Ⓐ cheering up
   - ● destruction
   - Ⓒ building
   - Ⓓ washing
5. If you act in a **foolhardy** way, you are ____
   - Ⓐ brave
   - Ⓑ sensible
   - ● reckless
   - Ⓓ thoughtful
6. The hermit crab **scuttles** about. This means it ____
   - Ⓐ hides under rocks
   - Ⓑ moves slowly
   - Ⓒ lumbers
   - ● scurries
7. If you are **efficient**, you ____
   - Ⓐ are extremely disorganized
   - Ⓑ never finish your work on time
   - ● waste no time doing the job
   - Ⓓ make a big mess when you work
8. Which of these might have **evolved**?
   - ● the use of computers
   - Ⓑ the chair you sit it
   - Ⓒ a flash of lightning
   - Ⓓ your lunch
9. Which word might go with **carcass**?
   - Ⓐ flower
   - Ⓑ grazing
   - Ⓒ plant
   - ● vulture
10. Which of these is not **secreted**?
    - Ⓐ tears
    - Ⓑ saliva
    - ● hair
    - Ⓓ sweat

106 Reading • EMC 4534 • ©2005 by Evan-Moor Corp.

Page 107

Skills: Understanding Word Meaning; Using a Dictionary; Drawing Conclusions

Write a Definition

Answer the questions using complete sentences. Use a dictionary if you need help.

1. What does the word **hermit** mean?

a person who lives alone away from others.

Why do you think the hermit crab was given its name?

It spends a lot of time hiding in its shell.

2. What does the word **carrion** mean?

dead, rotting flesh

Why do you think the carrion beetle was given its name?

It eats dead animals.

3. What does the word **invertebrate** mean?

without a backbone

Name an animal from the story that is an invertebrate.

carrion beetle, hermit crab, sponge, mite, fly, bee, anemone, ants, aphids

4. What does the word **prairie** mean?

flat, grassy land

Name an animal from the story that lives on the prairie.

bison or buffalo

©2005 by Evan-Moor Corp. • Reading • EMC 4534 107

Page 108

Skills: Critical Thinking; Categorizing

Types of Animals

Write the animal's name from the story under the correct heading. One category will have only two animals. Add a third animal.

ant, aphid, beetle, plover, cowbird, honey guide, bison, crab, sponge, anemone, honey badger

Bird	Insect
plover	beetle
cowbird	ant
honey guide	aphid

Mammal	Marine Invertebrate
bison	crab
honey badger	sponge
Answers will vary.	anemone

Create two animal headings of your own and list 3 animals under each heading.

Possible headings: Reptiles, Fish, Amphibians, etc.

108 Reading • EMC 4534 • ©2005 by Evan-Moor Corp.

Page 109

Skills: Identifying Correct Spelling; Writing Sentences

Which Spelling Is Correct?

Circle the correct spelling for each word.

appear	apear	appeer
crocadile	crockodile	**crocodile**
intresting	**interesting**	inersting
partical	**particle**	partacle
actually	acshually	actualy
poyson	**poison**	poisson
sevral	severel	**several**
emty	emptty	**empty**
camouflage	camoflage	cammoflage
farmiliar	**familiar**	fammiliar

Write sentences using the correct spellings of three words from the above list.

1. ______
2. ______
3. ______

©2005 by Evan-Moor Corp. • Reading • EMC 4534 109

Page 115

Skills: Recalling Details

Questions About The Sausage
A Story from Sweden

Fill in the circle that best answers each question.

1. At the beginning of the story, the woman was worried about her ______.
   - Ⓐ husband's clothing
   - ● husband's dinner
   - Ⓒ mother's health
   - Ⓓ milk cow
2. Who knocked at the door while the woman was making soup?
   - Ⓐ a tiny elf
   - Ⓑ a lost little boy
   - ● a strange old lady
   - Ⓓ a big hearty fellow
3. What did this person ask for?
   - Ⓐ something to ride on
   - Ⓑ something to wear
   - Ⓒ something to drink
   - ● something to eat
4. What did the kind woman give her visitor?
   - ● her last loaf of bread
   - Ⓑ her only pair of shoes
   - Ⓒ a glass of buttermilk
   - Ⓓ a bowl of homemade soup
5. Why did the husband wish the sausage on the end of his wife's nose?
   - Ⓐ He was upset because he was hungry and wanted something to eat.
   - ● He was mad because she had wasted a wish on the sausage.
   - Ⓒ He was mad at her for giving food to the old lady.
   - Ⓓ He had a headache that made him grumpy.
6. Why didn't the wife want to use the last wish to take the sausage off her nose?
   - Ⓐ She wanted to wish for a loaf of bread.
   - Ⓑ She liked having the sausage on her nose.
   - Ⓒ She wanted to wish for a new rocking chair.
   - ● She wanted her husband to wish for something he wanted.

©2005 by Evan-Moor Corp. • Reading • EMC 4534 115

Page 116

Skills: Critical Thinking; Getting the Main Idea

A Lesson to Learn

Traditional stories like this one often have a moral, or a lesson. What lesson do you think this story is trying to teach? Explain your answer.

Responses will vary, but may mention "think about your choices" or "put the good of others before your own gain."

Draw a picture to illustrate the moral of the story.

116 Reading • EMC 4534 • ©2005 by Evan-Moor Corp.

Page 117

Skills: Understanding Word Meaning

Choose the Right Meaning

Find each bolded word in the story and read the sentence in which it is found. Choose the correct meaning for the word.

1. The word **rustic** means ______.
   - ● countrified or rural
   - Ⓒ expensive
   - Ⓑ citified or urban
   - Ⓓ cheap
2. The word **isolated** means about the same as ______.
   - Ⓐ located on a good road
   - Ⓑ nearby and familiar
   - ● lonely and remote
   - Ⓓ next to an airport
3. In this story, the word **sliver** means ______.
   - ● a tiny slice
   - Ⓑ a big chunk
   - Ⓒ shiny and bright
   - Ⓓ plain and simple
4. The word **freshet** means about the same as ______.
   - Ⓐ handkerchief
   - Ⓒ basket
   - Ⓑ sausage
   - ● flood
5. The wife was **inconsolable** over her mistake. This means she was so upset that she ______.
   - Ⓐ turned blue in the face
   - Ⓑ got the hiccups
   - Ⓒ passed out
   - ● could not be comforted in any way
6. The word **evident** means about the same as ______.
   - Ⓐ sorry
   - Ⓒ hidden
   - ● obvious
   - Ⓓ difficult
7. He was paid a **meager** amount for his service. Meager means ______.
   - Ⓐ sufficient
   - Ⓒ plentiful
   - Ⓑ generous
   - ● small
8. Winter is **lingering** this year. Lingering means ______.
   - Ⓐ freezing cold
   - Ⓑ leaving
   - ● remaining
   - Ⓓ mild
9. Which behavior would be **scrimping**?
   - ● using only a few bits of the sausage
   - Ⓑ giving the sausage to the old woman
   - Ⓒ eating all of the sausage in a few bites
   - Ⓓ cutting the sausage into two large pieces
10. Which word is a synonym for **measly**?
    - Ⓐ ample
    - Ⓑ wormy
    - Ⓒ spotted
    - ● meager

©2005 by Evan-Moor Corp. • Reading • EMC 4534 117

Page 118

Skills: Using Vocabulary in Context

Which Word Fits?

Complete each sentence using a word from the story.

Word Box			
tramp	eccentric	anguish	famished
humble	timid	battered	exotic

1. Being a humble sort, the hero did not brag about his brave deeds.
2. The rare spices came from faraway lands and were very exotic.
3. We were quite exhausted after our long tramp through the woods.
4. The battered household furnishings had definitely seen better days.
5. His eccentric behavior earned him the reputation of town character.
6. The stray cat was famished and wolfed down the tuna we offered.
7. Maya is generally too timid to ask questions of the teacher.
8. The mother's anguish was great when it seemed that her child was missing.

118 Reading • EMC 4534 • ©2005 by Evan-Moor Corp.

Page 119

Skills: Using Apostrophes

Correct the Apostrophes

Apostrophes are used in contractions and to show possession.

it's = it is	what's = what is
Fido's chew bone	a bird's nest

Rewrite each sentence leaving out apostrophes that do not belong and adding apostrophes where they are needed.

1. My younger sisters pajama's were covered with flowers'.
   sister's
2. All the dishes' in the cupboard's were broken except for Sharons.
   Sharon's
3. We hope its going to be a sunny day on Saturday for Heathers picnic.
   it's Heather's
4. The kids' made a big mess in the front yard of the Johnsons house.
   Johnson's
5. Of all the horse's in the pasture, Wills is the prettiest.
   Will's
6. When Lydia saw Hildas new baby, she asked, "Whats its name?"
   Hilda's What's
7. Somebodys suitcases' were left in the trunk of Angelas' car.
   Somebody's Angela's
8. Shes going to be signing her book's at the mall next Tuesday.
   She's

©2005 by Evan-Moor Corp. • Reading • EMC 4534 119

Page 120

Skills: Using a Graphic Organizer; Working with Story Elements

Making a Story Map

Fill in each section of the story map by writing key words and phrases about each story element in "The Sausage." Using your story map as a guide, tell a friend or family member the story.

Setting
small cottage
isolated
forest
sunset

Characters
woman
husband—woodcutter
strange old lady in exotic clothes

Major Events
The woman gives her last loaf of bread to a strange old lady.
The old lady grants three wishes.
The woman wishes for a sausage.
The husband gets angry and wishes the sausage were on his wife's nose.

Conclusion
The husband used the last wish to wish the sausage off his wife's nose.

120 Reading • EMC 4534 • ©2005 by Evan-Moor Corp.

Page 129

Skills: Recalling Details; Drawing Conclusions

Questions About Baba Yaga

Fill in the circle that best answers each question.

1. Which word best describes Olga?
   - ● clever
   - Ⓑ stupid
   - Ⓒ timid
   - Ⓓ lazy
2. What do you think Olga's stepmother hoped would happen when she sent Olga to Baba Yaga's house?
   - Ⓐ She hoped Olga would get a needle and thread.
   - Ⓑ She hoped Olga would live happily with Baba Yaga.
   - ● She hoped Baba Yaga would do away with Olga.
   - Ⓓ She hoped Baba Yaga would give Olga some nice food.
3. Baba Yaga's hut was unusual because it had ______.
   - Ⓐ goat legs
   - Ⓑ frog legs
   - Ⓒ chicken wings
   - ● chicken legs
4. Baba Yaga sent the servant girl to draw water because she wanted to ______.
   - Ⓐ be kind to Olga
   - ● cook Olga in boiling water
   - Ⓒ help Olga wash her clothes
   - Ⓓ get Olga a cool drink after her long walk
5. How did Baba Yaga cope with the enchanted river?
   - Ⓐ She froze the river into ice and walked across it.
   - ● She drove her oxen to the river and made them drink it up.
   - Ⓒ She put a magic spell on the river that caused it to disappear.
   - Ⓓ She used an enormous sponge to soak up all the water in the river.
6. What was the happy ending to this story?
   - Ⓐ Olga went away to boarding school.
   - Ⓑ Olga found a giant ruby under her pillow.
   - Ⓒ Olga and her father moved to a new house.
   - ● Olga got a new stepmother who was kind and loving.

©2005 by Evan-Moor Corp. • Reading • EMC 4534 129

Page 130

Skills: Making Inferences; Making a Prediction; Critical Thinking

Write About the Story

Answer each question with complete sentences.

1. How did Baba Yaga's animals help Olga? Why did they do so?
   cat—took Olga's place at the loom so Olga could run away
   dog—let her leave.
   They helped because Olga had given them food.
2. How did Olga's father feel when he heard what had happened to Olga?
   He chased the wicked stepmother away.
3. What do you think happened to Olga's stepmother in the dark forest?
   Responses will vary.
4. We are told that the new wife was a loving stepmother in "word and deed." What do you think that phrase means?
   She both spoke and acted kindly toward Olga.

130 Reading • EMC 4534 • ©2005 by Evan-Moor Corp.

Page 131

Skills: Understanding Word Meaning

Choose the Right Meaning

Find each bolded word in the story and read the sentence in which it is found. Choose the correct meaning for the word.

1. The word **chastise** means to ____.
   - Ⓐ hug
   - ● scold
   - Ⓒ praise
   - Ⓓ forgive
2. The word **trickle** means ____.
   - Ⓐ a joke
   - Ⓑ a flood
   - ● a tiny stream
   - Ⓓ a kind of candy
3. The word **exertion** means ____.
   - Ⓐ expense
   - ● effort
   - Ⓒ ease
   - Ⓓ rest
4. If you are **vengeful**, you seek ____.
   - Ⓐ help
   - Ⓑ riches
   - Ⓒ safety
   - ● revenge
5. The stepmother's kindness was **pretense**. She was ____.
   - ● pretending
   - Ⓑ lazy
   - Ⓒ truthful
   - Ⓓ honest
6. The word **harrowing** means ____.
   - Ⓐ cold and uncomfortable
   - ● stressful and disturbing
   - Ⓒ delightful and exciting
   - Ⓓ dull and boring
7. If you thought your efforts were **futile**, you might feel ____.
   - Ⓐ happy
   - Ⓑ confused
   - ● hopeless
   - Ⓓ successful
8. A grin that is **menacing** is ____.
   - ● threatening
   - Ⓑ comical
   - Ⓒ inviting
   - Ⓓ cockeyed

Baba Yaga used an unusual form of transportation to chase Olga. It was a mortar and pestle. Find out what a mortar and pestle looks like and draw it here.

©2005 by Evan-Moor Corp. • Reading • EMC 4534 131

Page 132

Skills: Understanding Word Meaning from Context

Figure Out the Meaning

Use the context of the sentence to figure out the meaning of the **bolded** word. Write the meaning on the line.

1. The once trickling stream became a raging **torrent**.

   Torrent means rushing, wild water.
2. The staff at the hotel was extremely **solicitous** to our needs.

   Solicitous means attentive, helpful.
3. Don't be surprised if the children **lament** the loss of their pet for a long time.

   Lament means grieve, feel sad about.
4. His expression became a **grimace** when the knife slipped and he cut his finger.

   Grimace means expression of pain.
5. I ran into the table which **protruded** into the hallway.

   Protruded means stuck out.
6. We could tell that something was **amiss** the moment we entered the room.

   Amiss means wrong, not normal.

132 Reading • EMC 4534 • ©2005 by Evan-Moor Corp.

Page 133

Skills: Using a Graphic Organizer: Summarizing

Making a Story Map

Write a brief summary of the beginning, middle, and end of the story in the boxes on the left side. Then use the smaller boxes on the right to record three important details about each part of the story. Write your own response to the story in the bottom box.

Responses will vary.

Beginning Olga's cruel stepmother sent her to her sister's to fetch a needle and thread.	**Detail #1** The stepmother was mean when Olga's papa was not home. **Detail #2** The stepmother gave Olga a bundle of food. **Detail #3** Olga went into the forest.
Middle The sister was a witch and intended to eat Olga.	**Detail #1** Olga gave food to the witch's dog and cat. **Detail #2** Olga was kind to the servant girl. **Detail #3** The witch told Olga to work at her loom.
Ending Olga escaped and ran home.	**Detail #1** Baba Yaga's servant, cat, and dog helped Olga escape. **Detail #2** Her father chased the stepmother away. **Detail #3** Olga's father married a kind woman who was a loving mother.

Did you enjoy reading this story? Why or why not?

Responses will vary.

©2005 by Evan-Moor Corp. • Reading • EMC 4534 133